SCOTLAND'S FUTURE

SCOTLAND'S FUTURE

The Economics of Nationalism

By GAVIN McCRONE

AUGUSTUS M. KELLEY · PUBLISHERS
NEW YORK 1969

Published in the United States by

Augustus M. Kelley · Publishers

New York, New York 10001

678 06252 8

Library of Congress Catalog Card Number
71-92501

Printed in Great Britain

CONTENTS

ACKNOWLEDGEMENTS

I would like to thank Professor A. J. Brown and Mr Vivian Woodward of the National Institute of Economic and Social Research for kindly making available to me the estimates of gross domestic product and other variables from their regional accounts. I am also indebted to officials of the Scottish Office, the Inland Revenue, the Treasury and the Department of Economic Affairs for help with statistical information. But the responsibility for the use to which such material has been put and for the arguments advanced is entirely my own.

12 January 1969 Gavin McCrone

CHAPTER I

The Rise of Scottish Nationalism

At the moment of writing public opinion polls suggest that about a third of the Scottish electorate would vote for the National Party in an election. Some give them the largest share of the vote exceeding Conservative and Labour, others suggest approximately equal shares going to Nationalist and Conservative with Labour trailing some distance behind. If these forecasts are at all accurate a general election held at present could well see 15 or more Nationalist members elected to Parliament. This is a quite unprecedented situation in Scotland. The purpose of this essay is to consider how it arose and what its implications are.

Scottish nationalism is not new. The Scottish National Party has existed in one form or another since 1927 and there have been periods of considerable nationalist agitation before. An estimated two million people signed the Scottish Covenant in 1949, a document demanding a separate Parliament for Scotland within the framework of the United Kingdom. Before the First World War the Liberal Party, then in power, proposed to introduce home rule to Scotland in the same way as it intended for Ireland and as it remains pledged to do today. Between the wars too, strong feeling in Scotland led to the establishment of the various branches of the Scottish Office in St Andrews House in Edinburgh. What is new about the present situation is that the current wave of feeling seems likely to score some Parliamentary success and that the Scottish National Party, unlike the Covenant or many of the earlier movements, stands not for devolution or a federal constitution, but for independence and separation from England.

The party's success has been remarkably sudden. Though Dr. Robert MacIntyre, a nationalist, won Motherwell with a majority of 600 at a bye-election in 1945, the circumstances of the time were rather exceptional and he lost it again a few months later in the general election when Labour were returned with a majority of 8,000. After that no Scottish National Party candidate came near to winning a seat until the 1960s. The first straw in the wind was the bye-election for West Lothian in June 1962. Here the Labour candidate, Tam Dalyell, was returned with an immense majority of 11,500, but the Nationalist William Wolfe came second with 23 per cent of the poll, causing the Conservative, Liberal and Communist candidates all to lose their deposits. In the same way the total votes cast for the Scottish Nationalist candidates had been only 7,000 in the general election of 1951, 12,000 in 1955 and 21,000 in 1959; it then rose to 63,000 in 1964 and to 128,000 in 1966. But even this was a small figure in a country of some 3½ million voters and on neither of these occasions did they come within sight of winning a seat in Parliament. Events since then, however, have been dramatic. At the Pollock bye-election in the spring of 1967, a Conservative, Esmond Wright, won the seat from Labour, but the Nationalists made a strong impact and took 28% of the poll. Then at Hamilton in 1967 Mrs Ewing won the seat for the party with a majority of 2,000 and 46% of the poll. From then until the time of writing this momentum has continued. In the Scottish local elections of May 1968 the party made a major impact for the first time, capturing 100 seats, and winning around 30 per cent of the votes of the poll. As a result Labour lost control of Glasgow after a period of rule, which with the exception of one short break, had lasted more than thirty years. Similar results were obtained in Dundee and Aberdeen. All this has led up to a situation where, according to a party spokesmen, with present paid up membership of 127,000 the Scottish National Party is now the largest political party in Scotland.

There is no doubt that these achievements are impressive. But when set against what have come to be accepted views of British politics there are several respects in which they are particularly remarkable. In the first place there is no clearly defined leadership in the party. The electoral fortunes of Conservative or Labour parties are supposed to depend to a large extent on the talent and abilities of Mr. Heath and Mr.

Wilson and of the image of them that is created. But neither the president of the National Party, Dr. MacIntyre, nor the chairman, Mr. Donaldson, has made a strong impact and many Scots would have difficulty in saying who the leader of the party was. Much the same applies to policy. While the commitment to nationalisation of industry has sometimes been thought to be a hindrance to Labour at the polls, the Conservative failure to put forward an alternative to the economic policies followed by Labour from 1964 to 1968 has clearly been to their disadvantage. Yet Nationalist policies on such matters are far from clear. Combining as they do monarchists and republicans, supporters from the left, who wish to expropriate foreign companies and nationalise the land, with supporters from the right, it is by no means easy to reach agreement on the practicalities of domestic economic management. By degrees, and to their credit, they are gradually working out a consensus on some of these issues, though how long such unity would last when confronted with the responsibility of Government is at least open to question. The one issue of policy on which the position of the party is abundantly clear is that it stands for a completely independent Scotland. On this they are quite explicit. They are not working for devolution, or a Scottish parliament within a federal United Kingdom, as were the supporters of the 1949 Covenant. What they want is a sovereign independent Scotland with its seat at the United Nations, its own ambassadors, admirals and the rest.

One of the most remarkable features of the whole situation is that only a small part of the Scottish electorate seem to support this programme. Polls suggest that a majority of Scots may readily be found who think that Scotland should have a 'larger say in her own affairs', though, since no one likes the implication that he cannot run his own affairs, this is a somewhat emotive question unlikely to produce a negative response. A majority would probably favour the creation of a Scottish parliament and certainly the feeling is widespread that measures devised in Whitehall, such as selective employment tax and the Transport Bill, are unsuitable to Scotland's conditions. But all the evidence suggests that the proportion of Scots who wish to sever ties with England and set up a separate state is still small.

Why then is the National Party gaining so much support? Perhaps partly because votes cast for the party appear to be the most effective way of getting Government to pay attention to Scottish demands. Partly because, whatever the Nationalists say they stand for, many people believe that a Scottish parliament within the United Kingdom would be the compromise which would emerge after a large Nationalist vote at an election. It may be because the difference between home rule, or devolution, and independence is obscure to many people and is represented as one of degree. In fact it is no such thing; the difference is one of principle. Either Scotland is part of the United Kingdom enjoying political and economic union with England, or it is an independent state. There is no room for compromise.

But none of these explanations can alone account for the sudden growth of support for the party in the last two years. To understand this one has to take a wider view. Scotland is sometimes thought of as a traditional Labour stronghold, but this is hardly true except in recent years and there has never been the sort of Labour dominance that exists in Wales. Certainly there are large areas of heavy industry, where, as in the rest of Britain, Labour tends to get a high share of the vote. But as the figures below show, Labour had a majority over all other parties of only 3 in the Parliament of 1945 to 1950, though there was also a Communist and 4 ILP members. In 1950 they again had a majority of 3, Conservatives and Liberals having 34 seats for their 37. In 1951 the Conservatives gained power by a small margin at Westminster, while in Scotland the two parties had an exactly equal number of seats. From 1955 to 1959 the Tories had a majority, but in 1959, contrary to the trend in the United Kingdom, Labour gained four seats and an overall majority of five. This trend was repeated in 1964 and 1966. Indeed at this last election Labour gained a larger number of seats than it had ever before held in Scotland, nine more than in 1945 or 1929. The Tories had only 20 seats, nine less than in 1945 and equal to 1929. Never had they done so badly in

Scotland since the Liberal party ceased to be a major force.

Seats Gained at General Elections in Scotland

Pre-War

	1922	1923	1924	1929	1931	1935
Conservative	13	14	36	20	57	43
Liberal	27	22	8	13	7	3
Labour	29	34	26	37	7	20
Others	2	1	1	1	-	5

Post-War

	1945	1950	1951	1955	1959	1964	1966
Conservative	29	32	35	36	31	24	20
Liberal	-	2	1	1	1	4	5
Labour	37	37	35	34	38	43	46
Others	5	-	-	-	1	-	-

Though the National Party has never yet gained a seat at a general election in Scotland, there is no doubt that their support seems to come in cycles and that the periods in which they do best roughly correlate with times of Labour Government. Thus there was a wave in 1928-32 when the National party was founded; a second and stronger wave with the Scottish Covenant in 1949-51; and a third, stronger again, at the present time. In intervening periods of Tory rule, particularly during the 1950s, this support seems to ebb.

There is a good deal of dissatisfaction within the status quo in Scotland, and it may be that when in opposition, Labour, as allegedly the more reformist of the two major parties, is able to marshall this in its own support. Nationalisation, economic planning and the technological revolution are represented as the keys to the promised land. But when a period of office shows Labour's panaceas to be bankrupt, an alternative has to be found. The Liberals, whatever they may say they stand for, are thought of as occupying a moderate position between Conservative and Labour. It is the contented Scots who vote Conservative. Disillusion requires something more drastic, and nationalism is the obvious choice.

Thus the swing to Labour from 1959 to 1966, most of which was a period of Tory rule, is most commonly explained by referring to the poor performance of the economy. As a later chapter will show the Scottish economy did quite well up to 1955; the gap between Scottish and UK income was narrowing and unemployment, though still above the British average, was at its lowest ever figure in peacetime. All this suddenly changed in 1958 when the end of the post-war boom in shipbuilding and coal, industries which were heavily represented in Scotland, hit the economy hard. Incomes lagged and unemployment rose. Thus while in 1959 Labour's electoral hopes in the United Kingdom as a whole suffered from the apparent success of the Macmillan administration in running the economy, they gained in Scotland. Scotland's economic difficulties continued in the 1960's despite the improvements made to regional policy, and the Labour swing was repeated in 1964 and 1966. By then, however, Labour was in power and although, as will be shown later, they gave regional policy a higher priority than any previous government, they found it necessary to impose a long spell of deflationary and unpopular measures. Those who had swung to Labour in 1959 and 1964 had been enticed by the alternative economic policy it seemed to offer, and the prospect was held out that Scotland's problems could only be overcome by a party which wholeheartedly embraced economic planning and put an end to the stop-go cycle. Everyone knows how the failure of this alternative has produced widespread disillusion with Labour in England. In Scotland, however, this situation played right into the hands of the National Party. If there seemed little to distinguish Labour policy from Conservative, the National Party offered the only real alternative. Whatever the other parties might promise before an election, the National Party could be relied on to put Scotland's interests first. Conservative and Labour politicians might claim that nationalism would be economically disastrous for Scotland. But to the average Scot this seemed unconvincing at a time when these parties seemed quite incapable of managing the British economy, when Scotland's unemployment and emigration persisted despite 30 years of regional policy and Scotland's rate of economic growth over the ten year period 1955-65 was the lowest recorded in Western Europe. Could the Nationalists do worse than that?

On the political plane too the moment may seem more opportune than at any time in the past. Britain's role in the world is clearly changing. Whilst Britain was a world power, responsible for an empire, for keeping peace in the world and periodically threatened by other powers similar to her in size and strength, the break-up of the United Kingdom could have serious consequences. Today there seems much uncertainty about Britain's role in the world; but if Britain is going to opt out of this kind of responsibility entirely and play the part, say, of another Sweden, as some would wish her to do, then the political argument for a United Kingdom is reduced and Scotland may see itself as a second Norway.

These factors may go some way towards explaining the present situation. But they give little help in trying to predict whether the present wave of nationalism is a temporary phenomenon, a tartan Orpington, or whether it will grow in strength and have more lasting consequences. In the spring of 1967 at the Pollock bye-election, many of those who voted nationalist would have voted for one of the major parties in a general election, according to a poll taken at the time. To some extent that may still be true in 1968; but the situation has changed. In 1966 the party still had no major success to its credit, and to vote Nationalist was, like voting Liberal in many constituences, an elaborate way of abstaining and registering protest at the same time. At bye-elections, where the outcome will not affect the Government in power, the protest vote may therefore be quite strong; but at a general election under the British system the pressures to keep a particular party out of office are so strong that the minor parties are unlikely to hold their support except where they have demonstrated that they are capable of winning seats. In this respect the Nationalists were not a credible party in 1966, but it may be that now, in 1968 they are. Once a party can show that it is past this critical stage, its support may rapidly acquire momentum as more and more people realise that a vote cast for it is not a wasted vote. This is all the more likely to happen if the next general election turns out to be a walkover for one of the major parties. If the party to form the Government is a foregone conclusion, then there is no question of voting to keep a particular party out of office and the Scots may decide to vote Nationalist as a means of applying pressure in Westminster.

Probably the most important factor in predicting whether the National Party has any future is the position of Labour. The biggest source of support for the National Party has been disillusioned Labour voters. More than half their support is supposed to come from Labour voters and the seats they are most likely to win are for this reason in urban working class areas. Here the absence of a class image is a great asset to them. A disillusioned Labour docker will vote Nationalist where he would never vote Conservative or even Liberal without feeling he had betrayed his class; and the same applies to a disgruntled Tory duke. Much therefore depends on Labour's capacity to win back its support before the next election. If, as is predicted by all economic forecasters, devaluation and the 1968 budget start bringing the economy back into external balance in 1969, the unemployment level will fall, Bank Rate will come down and the tax burden may be eased. The Government may then be represented as having had the courage to stick to unpopular measures which paid off in the long run, and their support may recover to a remarkable extent. If events follow this pattern, the summer of 1968 may turn out to be the high tide of nationalism for the present and their support may start to ebb. If, on the other hand, the economy does not recover, or if its recovery is too slight, too long delayed or accompanied by further unpopular measures, then the National Party may gain further support.

If Scotland does go Nationalist, and shows herself anxious to leave the United Kingdom, she could hardly be denied the right to do so. The Union of 1707 was freely negotiated by the Parliaments of both nations. England needed political and strategic security from the north in an age when she was threatened from the Continent. Scotland wanted her economy to have access to English markets and to the English colonies then highly protected in an age of mercantilist trade policies. Both nations wanted an end to the long history of strife between them. There can be no doubt that the Union realised these advantages for both countries and that they both benefited enormously. Scotland, which was poor and one of the most backward states in Europe, enjoyed remarkable economic growth. It was perhaps no accident that it was a Scottish professor of moral philosophy, Adam Smith who became the father of economics and the great exponent of free trade. It was partly a consequence of the admitted success of the Anglo-Scottish union that a similar and much less successful union was made with Ireland in 1800. But the key to this success was that both countries were able to gain, not at each others expense, but because as one state there were some advantages which neither had individually. This is still the issue today. Surprising though it may seem south of the border after 260 years of union, a national consciousness still exists in Scotland. Scots think of themselves as different from English and are proud of their heritage, their history, their culture and their separate institutions in a way that does not apply to those who now inhabit the kingdoms of Mercia or Wessex. Most Scots would therefore regard it as essential that the Union continue to be of benefit to both countries. This does not mean that both countries should be in every respect identical, with the same rate of growth, standard of living, unemployment and so forth. After all, one of the purposes of economic union is to concentrate resources, whether they be capital or labour, in such a way that they yield the best return. But should it ever be clear that the union is working consistently to Scotland's disadvantage and that politically and economically she would be better off as a separate state, then many Scots might come to feel that their elected representatives should repeal the 1707 Act.

This then is the issue. Is Scotland in that position now? Many people approach this question by asking if Scotland could go it alone. An absurd question. Scotland has an income per head, which though slightly lower than that of England, still puts her among the more wealthy nations of the world. With a population of 5 million she would be a small state but larger than many others in Europe and elsewhere. She is better placed to afford independence, if she really wants it, than any of the countries of the British Empire which have become independent since the war. She has nothing like the economic or political problems which Ireland had to face. But the question which matters is whether separation would be to the advantage of the Scots or of Scotland. National parties in any country can of course always count on a certain amount of emotional support; and dwelling on the wrongs or the glories of past history may stimulate this. So some Scottish Nationalists may exploit the barbarities inflicted by England's King Edward on William Wallace or the battlecry of Bruce at Bannockburn. This is irrelevant to Scotland's future and dangerous in so far as it stirs up animosity between peoples who, whatever happens, have got to live together in these islands. In public debate the political and economic issues seem poorly understood. Few Scots seem to have a clear idea of the kind of Scotland which Nationalist policies would produce. Neither has the National Party given a convincing picture. Assertions abound about the state of Scotland's economy and its relation with England, but these are based on little factual evidence and a desire to fit what there is to the case being pleaded. There is a need, therefore, for a much better understanding of the issues which are at stake for the future of Scotland.

CHAPTER II

The Economy

As the last chapter has shown, recent political developments in Scotland are closely connected with the state of the economy. It is therefore necessary to have some understanding of the nature of Scotland's economic problems and of the changes that are required if they are to be overcome. There are a number of fallacies about the Scottish economy which it is necessary to dispel at the outset. At one extreme there are those south of the Border who sometimes appear to imagine their northern neighbour as a nation of crofters, dependent for their standard of living on agricultural subsidies, the whisky industry and American tourists. At the other there are an increasing number of Scots who have recently developed the habit of comparing their country with Scandinavia, and who therefore argue that Scotland has only to become independent for her economic problems to be resolved.

In reality Scotland is a highly urbanised and industrialised country. Though her land area comprises roughly a third of the United Kingdom, some seventy-five per cent of her population of 5 million is concentrated in the Central Lowlands. Indeed Glasgow and the surrounding Clydeside conurbation account for about 40 per cent of Scotland's population and a similar proportion of income, a degree of concentration greatly exceeding that of Greater London in the economy of England. Far from being a dominant activity, agriculture employs only 5 per cent of the working population and accounts for a similar proportion of the country's output. By international standards these are very low figures, making the Scottish economy less dependent on agriculture than any other nation in the world, save the United Kingdom itself. Much attention is focussed on the Highlands, and in particular on the Crofting Counties, where agriculture is a dominant form of activity. But though these counties account for some 40 per cent of Scotland's land area, their total population is only 280 thousand and their contribution to Scottish income only about 4 per cent.

There is a third fallacy about the Scottish economy, which is that it suffers from stagnation. This arises from a rather superficial look at the statistics for the overall growth rate. But far from being stagnant, it is a characteristic of the Scottish economy that it is undergoing drastic structural change; and this chapter will attempt to show that it is this necessary process which accounts for many of Scotland's economic difficulties.

Thus a high degree of concentration and urbanisation, a high level of industrialisation and an exceptional rate of structural change are the dominant economic characteristics of Scotland. Added to this are the extremely close economic relations which the country has had with England. It is against this background that Scotland's economic problems must be seen if they are to be understood.

Scotland's Economic Problems

The natural starting point for an assessment of a country's economic performance is to compute its national income or product. This is the sum of all incomes received from the production of goods and services in the economy. Without this it is impossible to find out how well off a country is, how its standard of living compares with that of other countries, or what progress its economy is currently making. No official estimate of these figures exists for Scotland, but in an earlier book I have computed the output of the Scottish economy over the period 1951-60. (1) The figure I calculated, gross domestic product, measures the output of the Scottish economy, but unlike national income it takes no account of income received by Scottish residents from elsewhere, nor does it deduct income arising in Scotland which is paid to shareholders and others living outside Scotland. Nevertheless this statistic gives an accurate measure of the Scottish economy's performance. It was found that Scotland's GDP in 1960 was 8.7 per cent of the United

Kingdom total. Expressed per head of the population, it measures the overall productivity of the economy; thus with a Scottish figure of £377 per head in 1960 compared with the United Kingdom's £431, Scotland's output per head was 88 per cent of the British average. Since the difference between GDP and national income is very small, this may be taken as a guide to the Scottish standard of living.

Very similar results are obtained from other sources. The surveys of personal income conducted by the Inland Revenue and the annual Family Expenditure Survey both estimate Scottish income per head at around 87-89 per cent of the United Kingdom average in the years 1959/60 and 1964/65. Personal income is, of course, a rather different concept from GDP, being limited to income accruing to individuals in Scotland and including investment income derived from assets held outside Scotland. But the conclusions are the same.

It is thus an incontestable fact that production and income per head of population are lower in Scotland than they are in Britain as a whole. From this it follows that tax yields, pro rata, are also lower, especially when levied at a progressive rate on incomes, and that, other things being equal, ability to finance public expenditure is also less, a question which is examined further in Chapter IV. However the difference between the Scottish and United Kingdom figures of GDP per head is not large, a mere 12 per cent or so. Moreover this compares with a similar figure for Wales and is well above Northern Ireland's GDP per head, which is currently only 65 per cent of the United Kingdom level. The Irish Republic's figure is even lower at around 55 per cent. No country can expect to have a uniform level of income or output per head throughout its length and breadth; and, with the exception of Northern Ireland, the regional variation is extremely small in Britain, especially when compared with countries like France or Italy. In sum, then, the figures show that Scotland is a relatively wealthy and advanced country, not quite so well off as England, but with a GDP per head 60% above the level of the Irish Republic and comparable to the levels prevailing elsewhere in Western Europe.

The best known and most spoken of feature of the Scottish economy is of course its unemployment. The percentage rate of unemployment has in many years been approximately double the United Kingdom average, but it was less than this in the years up to 1954 and it is also less than this now in 1968 when the UK figure is at its highest level since the war. To get this into perspective, it must be remembered that throughout the post-war period unemployment has been exceptionally low by historical standards or when compared with many other countries. The Scottish figure has varied between 2½ per cent and 4½ per cent of the labour force; and the aggregate number of persons out of work has varied between 50,000 and 135,000, a figure which was recorded in the worst year, 1963. Set against pre-war experience, when unemployment rarely fell below 12 per cent of the labour force and rose as high as 25 per cent in the 1930s, with rates of 40 per cent recorded in some industrial towns, it is clear that this is a different order of problem altogether. Moreover, it may be remembered that before the war informed opinion regarded 3 per cent unemployment as the lowest level it was practical to maintain. (2) Scotland's rate of unemployment has been similar to those prevailing in Wales and Northern England throughout much of the post-war period and, as will shortly be shown, much below the levels found in Northern Ireland or the Irish Republic.

Perhaps more serious than the unemployment, has been the rate of emigration from Scotland. The excess of emigrants over incomers to Scotland averaged about 25,000 a year in the 1950s. This was the highest rate of net outflow of any region in Great Britain and equalled about half the population's rate of natural increase. However since 1960 it has become very much worse, rising to 40,000 in 1963/4 and reaching the post-war maximum of 47,000 in 1965/66. At this rate it exceeds the population increase, so that, since 1963/64 for the first time since the 1920s, there has been a net fall in the Scottish population. Moreoever much of this is a loss not only to Scotland but to Britain, in the years 1960-1965 65 per cent of this outflow went to England and Wales, the remainder going overseas.

Clearly all these problems, the level of income, unemployment and emigration give reason for concern. Moreover they all stem from the same cause, an insufficient rate of economic growth. Each of the problems cited above is evidence of spare capacity. Growth is needed to increase productivity and raise income, and to provide the new jobs which would reduce unemployment and emigration.

To assess a country's economic performance over a period it is necessary to have some sort of national income or product estimates over a number of years. This is the only means of calculating the rate of growth for the economy as a whole, and the absence of official figures of this type is therefore a serious gap in our information. Up to 1960 however the position is fairly clear. Professor Campbell's estimate of national income from 1924 to 1949 showed that Scotland lagged behind the United Kingdom in the interwar years and average income per head fell to about 86 per cent of the British average in the 1930s. (3) During the wartime expansion, however, much of this was made good and Scottish national income per head rose to 94 per cent of the British level in 1944 and 91 per cent in 1948. My own estimates of Scottish gross domestic product, already referred to, cover the period 1951 to 1960; these showed that Scotland's economic growth more or less kept pace with the United Kingdom up to the mid 1950s. In the latter half of the 1950s, however, it lagged seriously behind. Between 1954 and 1960 Scottish GDP grew only 10 per cent compared with 18 per cent growth for the United Kingdom, itself the slowest growing country in Western Europe. As a result, Scottish GDP per head had fallen from 92 per cent of the United Kingdom level in 1951 to 88 per cent in 1960. The growth of employment during this time was equally unsatisfactory, the total number employed in Scotland in 1960 being very slightly less than in 1954 and only 1.4 per cent above the 1950 figure. There is therefore no doubt that in every way the second half of the 1950s was a period of thoroughly unsatisfactory performance for Scotland, the causes of which will be discussed later in this chapter.

The position in the 1960s is much more complicated. Although there is no continuous series of national income or GDP estimates, there are a number of indications that the Scottish economy did much better in the 1960s than it did in the latter half of the 1950s. The index of industrial production compiled by the Scottish Office which covers manufacturing, mining, construction and power, in all about 48 per cent of GDP, shows Scotland with a very slightly higher growth between 1960 and 1966 than the United Kingdom, though not as high as Northern Ireland. The Ministry of Labour Earnings Enquiries also show an encouraging trend: whereas weekly earnings of male manual workers in industry in Scotland were 91 per cent of the British average in 1961 they rose steadily during the 1960s and reached 97.2 per cent in 1967. Similar evidence is obtained from the Family Expenditure Surveys. These showed that while income per household in Scotland was only 92 per cent of the British average in 1961/2 it had risen to 96 per cent in the years 1965/67. Owing to the larger size of household in Scotland, this gives income per head figures at 87 per cent of the British average in 1961/2 and 89 per cent in 1965/7.

On the other hand Scotland's growth of employment during these years was less satisfactory. Employment growth was better than in the 1950s when, as has been shown above, it was almost negligible; but Scottish employment in 1966 was only 3 per cent above 1960 compared with 6 per cent in the United Kingdom as a whole, 5 per cent for Wales and 6.6 per cent for Northern Ireland. It was no doubt partly in consequence of this that the Scottish emigration figures were so high. It is clear, therefore, that while there are many indications that the income per man employed was rising in Scotland to nearer the British average, the number employed in Scotland as a proportion of total British employment continued to fall from 9.3 per cent in 1960 to 9.0 per cent in 1967.

In order to assess the significance of these trends, it is necessary to make an estimate of Scottish gross domestic product for a more recent year. Accordingly, my table below gives figures for 1964 and 1965, (the latest years for which sufficient Inland Revenue data was available) along with my earlier figure for 1960 and the National Institute estimate for 1961. It was not possible to prepare these new figures with the degree of precision obtained in the earlier estimates for the 1950s. and they must therefore be regarded as approximate only. While my estimate for 1960 was mainly computed by adding the output of each industry, the new estimates for 1964 and 1965, like the National Institute figure for 1961 are based on the sum of incomes. Of course the two approaches should give the same results, but it is possible that the difference of method introduces some lack of comparability. The 1961 estimate is directly comparable with those for the two later years except that it does not include the pay of armed forces overseas. But the main problem with these figures is that the total absence in the 1960s of a Census of Production. The main reason is that the total absence in the 1960s of a Census of Production containing Scottish figures makes any estimate of GDP for a recent year difficult. The latest Census containing Scottish figures at the time of writing (1968) is ten years old, something which must be regarded as no less than a scandal. Thus while income from employment and income from self-employment may be built up from Inland Revenue data, the absence of a Census compels recourse to some rough and ready procedures for the estimation of company profits. This situation of course is not alone in affecting GDP estimates, the absence of a Census may also affect the accuracy of the official Index of Industrial Production.

Fortunately company profits are a relatively minor component of GDP, so that, even allowing for a substantial margin of error in their estimation, the accuracy of the total GDP figure is unlikely to be greatly affected. There are, therefore, a number of conclusions which may be drawn. Scottish GDP per head in 1964 was about 87 per cent of the U.K. level, a similar percentage to that in 1960 and better than in 1961; in 1965 it rose slightly to 88 per cent. The tendency for this figure to fall as a percentage of the United Kingdom was therefore halted. However this is partly

Growth of Industrial Production

1960 = 100

	Scotland	N. Ireland	Wales	United Kingdom
1962	103	107	103	102
1964	114	124	118	113
1966	121	135	-	118
1967	119	142	-	118

Growth of Employment

1958 = 100

	Scotland	N. Ireland	Wales	United Kingdom
1950	99.2	102.8	96.0	95.1
1954	100.8	103.2	97.8	98.1
1960	100.6	106.3	101.6	103.0
1964	101.8	109.0	105.8	107.0
1966	102.8	113.3	106.6	109.0
Growth 1950–66 as %	3.6	10.2	11.1	14.8

GDP per head as % of U.K. average

	Scotland	N. Ireland	Wales
1948	91*	-	81
1951	92	65	84
1954	91	62	91
1960	88	63	90
1964	87	65	91

* National Income

achieved because the Scottish population was falling as a proportion of the total British population. Taking Scotland's GDP in aggregate, whereas this was 8.7 per cent of the British total in 1960, it had fallen to 8.4 per cent by 1964. Thus though Scottish living standards kept approximately in step with the United Kingdom, this was partly due to the outflow of population. The rate of growth of the Scottish economy in the first few years of the 1960s seems to have been slightly below that of the United Kingdom, being insufficient to maintain Scottish GDP in line with the United Kingdom, but there is some evidence of catching up after 1964.

The main reason for this was the failure of Scottish employment to expand faster. As a result Scottish income from employment, by far the biggest component of GDP, fell from 8.6 per cent of the United Kingdom total in 1960 to 8.3 per cent in 1964.

The figure given here contrasts rather sharply with an estimate of Scottish GDP in 1966 published by the *Scotsman.* (4) According to this estimate Scottish GDP in 1966 was £2,860 million or 8.8 per cent of the United Kingdom figure. This gave a GDP per head of £551.0 as compared with the United Kingdom's £596.3, a ratio of 92 per cent. Even allowing for the difference in the year, it is hard to reconcile this figure with our own estimates and, in view of the slow growth of Scottish employment, it would seem that the *Scotman's* figure must be too high.

One of the more surprising features to emerge from the statistics is that labour productivity in Scotland's industrial sector rose faster than in Britain during the 1960s. Attention was drawn to this in the Government's white paper, *The Scottish Economy 1965-70,* where the annual productivity increase in Scottish industry was estimated at 3.6 per cent compared with 3.1 per cent in the United Kingdom as a whole. (5) This is also apparent in our figures, in so far as the rate of employment growth in Scotland was significantly less than in the United Kingdom, although industrial output, as measured by the official index (Table 1) grew very slightly faster. It is somewhat ironical that Scotland should have so much success in raising labour productivity at a time when

TABLE II

SCOTTISH GROSS DOMESTIC PRODUCT

	1960	1961*	1964	1965
Income from Employment	1,309	1,340	1,606	1,745
Income from Self Employment	197	219	239	260
Gross Profits)		319	387	404
Gross Trading Surplus and) Surpluses of Public)	458			
Enterprise)		63	95	101
Rent)		102	128	151
GDP at factor cost** (excluding stock appreciation)	1,964	2,043	2.455	2.661
as a % of U.K.	8.7	8.4	8.4	8.5
GDP per caput: Scotland	£ 377	£ 395	£ 472	£ 511
U.K.	£ 431	£ 459	£ 542	£ 578
Scotland as %	87.5	86.1	87.0	88.4

*Estimate prepared by V. H. Woodward for a study being produced by National Institute of Social and Economic Research. Unlike the other years these figures do not include income of forces stationed abroad.

**No allowance for stock appreciation is deducted.

she had spare labour resources and needed more employment. But it is probably this rise in productivity which enabled earnings per man employed to rise closer to the British average as has already been shown. The reason for this will be discussed at greater length later on, but it is clear that the changes which were taking place in Scotland's economic structure offer the main explanation.

While there are many indications, therefore, that Scotland has certainly been doing much better in the 1960s than she did in the latter half of the 1950s, her performance is still some way short of adequate. If the unemployment and emigration are to be reduced, Scotland must aim at a rate of growth which is well and truly above the British rate.

Before leaving this subject, it is perhaps worth contrasting Scotland's performance with that of some other parts of the United Kingdom for which there are figures and with the Republic of Ireland, whose economy offers some interesting points of contrast.

Wales has somewhat similar income levels to Scotland, but it has enjoyed a better rate of growth in the last twenty years. Welsh GDP rose faster than that of the United Kingdom from 1948 to 1954, and from then onwards it has more or less kept pace. Thus GDP per head which was only 81 per cent of the British level in 1948 rose to 91 per cent in 1964. Welsh unemployment was in most years a slightly lower percentage than in Scotland, and although there was net emigration in the 1950s, this was at a much lower rate and has ceased in the 1960s.

Northern Ireland has a much lower income per head than Scotland, only 65 per cent of the United Kingdom average, and consistently the highest unemployment rate in the British Isles, varying between 6 and 8 per cent in recent years. The rate of economic growth was particularly low in the early 1950s, below the Scottish or British rates. Since then, however, the economy has made substantial progress and the rate of growth in the later 1950s and during the 1960s has outstripped the United Kingdom. The GDP per head therefore rose from 61 per cent of the United Kingdom level in 1958 to 65 per cent in 1964. The growth of employment has been less satisfactory, but substantially faster than in Scotland.

The Republic of Ireland provides in many ways the most interesting comparison, because there are so many points of contrast with Scotland. In 1965 gross national product at factor cost was £308 per head compared with £375 in Northern Ireland, £486 in Scotland and £578 for the

United Kingdom. This is therefore a lower figure than for any part of the United Kingdom, only 53 per cent of the British average and 63 per cent of the Scottish figure. The Irish price structure is somewhat different from the British, but, even so, this indicates the much lower standard or living in the Republic. Unemployment was 6.9 per cent of the insured employees in 1967 and has normally been somewhat lower than in Northern Ireland, though much above the levels in Scotland or any other part of the United Kingdom. Emigration is, of course, the traditional Irish problem and the flow of emigrants was at such a rate that the population fell steadily for a hundred years after 1841. From a peak of 8 million during the 1840s, or 6½ million in the counties of the present Republic, the population has fallen to 2.8 million in the Republic and 1.5 million in Northern Ireland. Apart from a few years in the late 1940s, when there was a modest population increase, this decline has only been reversed in the 1960s. This is emigration on an infinitely worse scale than Scotland has ever suffered, even if it has at last begun to subside just as Scotland's has become more serious.

Economic growth was likewise very poor until recently. Indeed during the 1950s up to 1958 Ireland's growth of GNP at constant prices was less than 1 per cent a year. Since then however there has been a remarkable improvement and GNP at constant prices had grown 33 per cent between 1958 and 1966. Undoubtedly this is largely due to Ireland's much improved economic policy since 1958. Only since then has the Irish Government given economic growth a high priority and instituted a system of incentives and economic planning to encourage it. The results, when compared with Ireland's past economic history, are certainly a great achievement; and they have not been lost on the Scottish National Party who sometimes seek to argue that they demonstrate the advantages of political independence.

But creditable though Ireland's growth has certainly been in the last ten years, it must be seen in perspective. Ireland's growth of 33 per cent is only marginally higher than that of the United Kingdom whose GNP rose 30 per cent between 1958 and 1966. It is a better rate of growth than Scotland achieved, though slightly less than Northern Ireland. It is, however, important to understand the shortcomings of this league table approach. A rate of growth depends not only on the amount of new development taking place but on the level of GNP in the base year. A given amount of new development will naturally appear as a much higher rate of growth if the base year GNP is low than if it is high. Thus although Ireland's *rate* of growth was faster than Scotland's in the ten years 1958 to 1968, this does not mean that the amount of new development in aggregate terms was larger in Ireland. Indeed Scotland's GDP at current prices rose £762 million between 1958 and 1965 compared with a rise of £362 million for the Irish Republic, which gives an increase per head of £146 in Scotland compared with £127 for Ireland. Thus, unless Scottish prices rose substantially faster than Irish, it is clear that in *absolute* terms, though not in *rate* Scotland's per caput growth was greater than Ireland's. Yet this was a period when Ireland's growth was much faster than ever before and Scotland's rather slow. Indeed apart from the *rate* of growth it is clear that in most other respects the Scottish economy is far better placed than the Irish.

While intercountry comparisons of this type show up many points of contrast, a true assessment of a country's economic performance demands an understanding of the circumstances in which the economy had to operate. Thus the problems of the Irish and Scottish economies are totally different. Ireland's economy is still dominated to a great degree by agriculture and one of the objects of policy is to bring about industrialisation. Scotland's economy is already heavily industrialised and her problems arise in large measure from the decline of industries which formed the basis of her prosperity in the past. To understand the nature of Scotland's economic problem properly, therefore, it is necessary to examine the structure of the economy, analysing the contribution of different sectors to the country's output and assessing their performance individually.

Scotland's Economic Structure

Some aspects of Scotland's economic structure have already been referred to at the start of this chapter, in particular the relatively small part played by agriculture. This is of course one of the striking features of the British economy, both Scotland and England. Agriculture, forestry and fishing together contributed 5.8 per cent of Scottish gross domestic product in 1960, compared with 4.0 per cent for the United Kingdom, and the proportions of the working population engaged in this sector were similar. Figures for other countries are normally much higher; in Germany, for instance, agriculture employs 10 per cent of the labour force and contributed 5 per cent GDP, in France the figures were 19 per cent and 9 per cent, in Ireland 35 per cent and 22 per cent and in Denmark 16 per cent of both GDP and labour.

Scottish agriculture by these standards is a relatively unimportant sector, but it still plays a larger part in the economy than it does in England. Owing partly to the high proportion of hill land, it is more heavily subsidised than British agriculture generally. The subsidy bill in recent years has been running around £40–45 million compared with £250–270 million for the United Kingdom, although the output is only some 12 per cent of the British total. But it is not as heavily subsidised as in Northern Ireland, and judged by the level of output per man employed, the level of efficiency is high by European standards. Productivity is twice or three times the German, French or Italian levels and roughly comparable to that found in Denmark or Holland. Such global figures, of course, conceal a wide variation around the average, and there is no doubt that, owing to the very varied nature of Scotland's terrain, there are tremendous differences in the effectiveness of her agriculture from one area to another. But the general impression is certainly of a highly capitalised, efficient industry.

As in other countries, however, the employment in Scottish agriculture is constantly falling. Though output has risen some 20 per cent since the mid-1950s, an exceptionally high rate of increase in labour productivity has enabled a steady outflow of agricultural labour to take place. Approximately 115,000 people are now engaged in Scottish agriculture and this has been falling at a rate of about 5,000 a year. Because the industry is slightly more important in Scotland than it is in the British economy generally, this outflow forms a larger proportion of Scottish employment than it does in the United Kingdom. Scotland's forestry and fishing comprises a much larger share of these industries in Britain than does agriculture, the employment being about a third of the British total; but in neither case is the employment large, nor is there a serious decline.

Like agriculture, coal mining has a declining labour force, but in this case there has also been a substantial fall in output in the last ten years. This industry too is more heavily represented in Scotland than it is in the United Kingdom as a whole but the difference is now small. In 1960 it contributed 3.2 per cent of Scottish GDP compared with 3.0 per cent in the United Kingdom as a whole. It is certainly of nothing like the importance to the Scottish economy that it is to the Welsh, where it accounts for about 10 per cent of GDP. Scottish coal-mining is also markedly less efficient than that of the United Kingdom generally. Output per man shift is currently only 1.59 tons compared with a British average of 1.82 and net output per man in 1960 was only 80% of the United Kingdom figure. As a result the Scottish division of the National Coal Board managed to make a small profit on operating costs only in 1963 and 1964 and when payment of interest on capital is considered has made a loss every year since 1949. During the last ten years there has been a steady contraction both in the output and the employment of the industry, for the same reasons as this has occurred in the United Kingdom and indeed in all Western European countries. Owing to the particularly unprofitable nature of the Scottish industry, this contraction has taken place rather more rapidly there than in Britain as a whole. Indeed Scottish output fell from 21 million tons in 1956, to 15 million tons in 1967, a decline of almost 30 per cent, while in the United Kingdom the fall was from 207 million tons to 167 million tons, a fall of 20 per cent. During the same period employment in Scottish mines fell from 84 thousand to 44 thousand a reduction of nearly half and a substantial proportion of the labour force to absorb and redeploy. Indeed this gives some indication of the scale of the structural readjustment the Scottish economy has been having to undergo since the mid 1950s. As far as coal mining is concerned, it is clear that this process will continue, but the rate of decline in the labour force is now likely to diminish as the remainder is concentrated on more efficient pits. In this sense the worst of the readjustment must now be past, and indeed it can hardly be otherwise for a continuation of the rate of decline experienced in the last decade would reduce the labour force approximately to zero in another ten.

Manufacturing is, of course, the most important single sector of the economy. Its contribution to the total output of the Scottish economy as measured by its share of Gross Domestic Product was 36 per cent in 1960, a figure similar to that of the United Kingdom; the proportion of employment is somewhat less (see Table III). The composition of manufacturing output is, however rather different from that of the United Kingdom. As the table shows, shipbuilding, textiles and metal industries, all of which are either declining or slow growing sectors, are more heavily represented in Scotland than in Britain; on the other hand, fast growing sectors, such as chemicals and vehicles, are under-represented by comparison.

This level of disaggregation is, of course, insufficient to show up many of the most important structural differences. Indeed one of the more surprising features of this Table is that, when broken down in this way, Scottish manufacturing employment is still much closer to that of the United Kingdom in composition than that of Wales, where metal industries predominate, or Northern Ireland, where textiles, shipbuilding and engineering account for the largest part. This may be because Scotland is larger than either of these other areas and therefore more self-contained. But of course this does not mean that the Scottish economy is simply a scaled down version of the United Kingdom's. If the differences are not as obvious as might be expected, this is because they occur to a large extent within sectors. Thus the 'vehicles' industry may comprise railway locomotives, cars or aeroplanes; 'textiles' range from linen, wool, jute and cotton to man-made fibres; 'food, drink and tobacco' include whisky, beer, mineral waters etc.; and the parts of these industries which are strongly represented in Scotland may differ substantially from the United Kingdom pattern. A closer examination confirms that this is the case, as the Toothill Committee found.(6) I have attempted to assess the importance of this in a previous book where I found that the effects of an adverse composition on growth were particularly marked in the Scottish chemicals, engineering, vehicles, and metal goods industries.(7) Scottish engineering specialised in trades which were affected by the decline in shipbuilding, and only in recent years has motor car production formed part of the Scottish vehicles industry.

An adverse structure is, therefore, of the utmost importance in accounting for the slow growth of employment in Scottish manufacturing industry. Indeed my earlier study shows that in the 1960s, though not in the 1950s, many of the growing industries and trades were actually growing faster in Scotland than in the United Kingdom as a whole. But for the heavy representation of shipbuilding, textiles and metal manufacture and the adverse composition within other sectors, therefore, Scotland might even have outperformed the United Kingdom in the rate of employment growth in the 1960s.

The remainder of the economy may be classified as service industries of one kind or another. Together they account for about 53 per cent, or just over half, the Gross Domestic Product. But although this is a very large share, there are fewer features which distinguish the role they play in Scotland from that which they fill in the United Kingdom generally. The main exception to this is transport and communication, which because of Scotland's land area, play a larger part in the Scottish economy than in Britain as a whole. Moreover, railways form an important part of this sector, and one which, since the end of the 1950s, has been contracting all over Britain as services have been closed. But once again Scotland, with its high proportion of services in areas of sparse population, has suffered from a more rapid contraction than Britain as a whole and therefore a sharper reduction in employment. As regards the other sectors, both construction and distribution appeared to have a much lower output per man in Scotland than in Britain generally in 1960, the difference being

TABLE III

(a) *Percentage of Labour Force Engaged in Selected Sectors*

	Scotland	United Kingdom	West Germany	France	Sweden	Ireland
Agriculture, forestry and fishing	5	3	10	19	14	35
Mining	2	2	2	2	1	1
Manufacturing	31	35	37	27	34	17
Services and other sectors	62	60	31	52	51	47

(b) *Percentage of Employees in Selected Manufacturing Industries*

	Scotland	Wales	N. Ireland	United Kingdom
Food, drink and tobacco	11.2	5.1	17.2	8.1
Chemicals	5.0	8.8	2.9	6.2
Metal Manufacture	8.8	35.7	-	8.5
Engineering & electrical	28.1	16.8	20.0	28.3
Shipbuilding	9.0	0.1	10.5	3.2
Vehicles	7.0	6.7	6.7	11.7
Metal goods	3.3	6.7	2.0	6.2
Textiles	7.4	5.1	22.9	6.1
Other	19.7	15.0	17.8	21.7
	100	100	100	100

around 15 per cent. Gas, electricity and water showed a slightly higher output per man, probably as a result of the capital intensive nature of hydroelectric production. Scotland's growth of employment in many of the service industries, notably distribution, finance and professional services, was slower during the 1960s than in the United Kingdom, but this probably reflects the virtual absence of growth in Scotland's population, and hence a slow increase in demand for these services.

Scotland's economic structure is, therefore, of great importance in accounting for her economic difficulties. It is not possible to quantify this very precisely, but the following figures which show the labour loss in some of the principal sectors where employment was declining give some idea of its importance (Table IV). In these sectors alone employment fell by 188,000 in thirteen years or by about 8 per cent of the Scottish working population. The full effect is obviously much larger than this; not only are the sectors listed here only those in which the decline was particularly striking, but there are important linkage effects in the economy which cause the decline in, say shipbuiling, to affect numerous component and related industries in greater or lesser degree.

TABLE IV

Approximate Loss or Employment 1954–67

Agriculture, Forestry and Fishing	–43,000
Mining and Quarrying	–42,000
Manufacturing:	
Textiles	–30,000
Shipbuilding	–19,000
Metal	–13,000
Locomotive & Carriage (vehicles)	–13,000
Transport & Communication:	
Railways	–28,000
	–188,000

Several important consequences follow from this. Given an adverse economic structure, it is obviously difficult to keep Scotland's rate of growth, whether of output or of employment, up to the United Kingdom average. The growing sectors have to make good the contraction in the declining sectors before they make any net contribution to the expansion of Scottish output or employment. Indeed, given the relatively greater importance of the declining sectors in Scotland and the smaller importance of the growing sectors than in Britain as a whole, Scotland's growth rate can only be kept up to the United Kingdom rate if the growing sectors grow much faster in Scotland than they do in Britain as a whole. If Scotland is to catch up the United Kingdom in income levels and to reduce its unemployment and emigration, then the growing sectors have to do even better than that.

To achieve a satisfactory growth of output, however, though difficult with an adverse structure, is much easier than to get an adequate growth of employment. In the first place there are many more industries which have declining employment than have declining output. Agriculture, textiles and metal manufacture, for example, have all achieved a growth of output over the last ten years although their employment has declined. Secondly many of the modern growth industries happen to be highly capital-intensive, while the old declining industries were mostly labour-intensive. For example, to produce a given value of output in coal mining or traditional textiles gave employment to a much larger number of men than the production of output to the same value does in electronics or chemicals. Thus, if the growing sectors expand fast enough to make good the loss in output from the declining industries, they may still fail to make good the loss in employment. This is probably the main reason why the growth of employment in Scotland during the 1960s has been so very much less satisfactory than the growth of output as shown by the index of industrial production.

But it would be a mistake to dwell only on the gloomy side of this structural question. The change in Scotland's economic structure is, of course, greatly to be welcomed; and as the declining industries gradually play a smaller part in the economy, so it will become easier to secure a satisfactory rate of growth in output and employment in Scotland. Already the worst may be over in this respect, for while decline will continue, the coal and shipbuilding industries are unlikely to run down as rapidly in the next decade as they did in the last. If they do, there will be hardly anything left of them. But the change in its economic structure also provides Scotland with a great opportunity. The replacement of old labour-intensive industries with modern capital-intensive growth may result in inadequate employment growth, but it results in a very satisfactory rise in labour productivity in Scotland. This makes possible an increase in earnings per man employed, and, as has been seen, this was occurring during the 1960s. Moreover the rise in labour productivity means that Scotland has the labour resources to achieve a much higher rate of growth than England, whose growth of output has been limited by shortage of labour resources and an inability to achieve a faster growth of productivity per man.

The Origin of the Problem

The statistics used so far have revealed some important facts crucial to a proper understanding of the Scottish economy. But these are little more than the bare bones. It is necessary now to ask how the Scottish economy got into this situation.

It is well known that Britain achieved remarkable economic success in the late 18th and throughout the 19th centuries. She became the first nation to industrialise and this was to have a number of important consequences. Thanks to the Act of Union in 1707, Scotland shared, and indeed took a leading part in, this tremendous expansion. The Union automatically gave Scotland the right of free trade both with England and with the English overseas territories; and she had herself both iron ore and coal, the resources on which success in the early part of the industrial revolution depended. Being the first nation to industrialise meant that for a time Britain had more or less a world monopoly in the sale of certain types of manufacture. She therefore expanded her output far beyond her own requirements and found it greatly to her interest to follow a world free trade policy. By importing cheap foodstuffs she gave other countries the income necessary to buy her exports of manufactures and at the same time kept her own cost of living low. This enabled labour costs and the prices of her manufactures to be kept down so that they were both within the means of other countries to buy and difficult for competitors abroad to match. But as a result of this, British agriculture, despite the substantial progress it had made and its relatively efficient structure resulting from the Acts of Enclosure, had to face extremely stiff competition, especially after 1870 when imports of grain began to come in large quantities from North America. The area of cultivated land in Britain, therefore contracted in the latter part of the nineteenth century; the output of many products was reduced, and, with the simultaneous expansion of industry, there was a constant movement of population out of agriculture. This process continued only with a short interruption for the First World War until the 1930s, when measures to support agriculture were started. By the end of this time home agriculture was supplying only about a third of Britain's food requirements, and the country had the smallest proportion of her population in agriculture of any nation in the world. But the more inefficient types of agricultural production had been wiped out and what remained was a relatively efficient industry.

The other side of this picture was that Britain's export industries were tremendously expanded. The coal industry with an output of 287 million tons in 1913 exported 73 million. At one stage towards the end of the 19th century, eighty per cent of the world's ships were built in Britain; the textile industries likewise were exporting a high proportion of their output. At the time this policy was followed it made excellent sense. Britain was concentrating her productive effort on those goods which she could produce most efficiently and importing those which could be obtained most cheaply abroad. This was the foundation of British prosperity and it was largely because of this that the British standard of living remained above that of the large Continental countries until the mid 1950s.

For other countries it was not so easy to follow this system. Different laws of land inheritance resulted in a more fragmented agricultural structure and, far from having a near monopoly of export markets for manufacturers as Britain had had, other nations had to fight their way into these markets against British competition. As a result industry had to depend more heavily on the home market of which the rural population was at that time a large part, and Continental farms with their fragmented holdings were even less able to withstand competition from the New World. As a result both France and Germany returned to agricultural protection in the 1870s. This maintained in those countries a much higher degree of self-sufficiency than in Britain; it enabled the less efficient farming units to survive and the agricultural population remained a substantial proportion of the labour force.

The British policy worked very well until the First World War. But in the inter-war period a number of factors caused it to break down. Other countries increasingly developed their own industries, so replacing the ships and the textiles they had bought from Britain. An overvalued exchange rate for the £ after the return to the gold standard in 1925 hit the export industries by pricing their goods out of foreign markets. When this was altered in 1931, the world depression and the emergence of protective trading blocs had even more disastrous effects. On top of all this there was a secular shift in demand away from the products of the old nineteenth century industries towards the motor vehicles, electrical goods and other new industries which were rapidly springing up.

As a result Britain's traditional export industries, shipbuilding, iron and steel, textiles, coal, went through a long period of depression which intensified in the 1930s, and those areas in which these industries were concentrated were hit particularly hard. Exports of coal fell from 79 million tons in 1923 to 39 million in 1933 and the national unemployment rates in the coal industry, in shipbuilding and in textiles were all very high. The areas most heavily hit were South Wales where unemployment reached 36 per cent of the labour force and the north of England where it was 29. Scotland was also hard hit with an unemployment rate which reached 28 per cent in 1932; but there was a much more rapid reduction thereafter than in Wales. Individual towns of course recorded phenomenally high rates.

It is hard to say how much of this was due to the long-term factors just described and how much was simply due to the slump. In so far as it was the latter, it would disappear when the economy as a whole returned to full capacity working. If it was long-term it would not. In the event the war intervened and the widespread destruction, particularly sinking of ships, and the dislocation to world trade, ensured full capacity working in all Britain's industries so that national unemployment fell to the record low figure of 25,000 in 1944. After the war, as the next chapter will show, an active regional policy was pursued for some years which brought a substantial amount of new industry to Scotland, northern England and Wales; but at the same time post-war shortages ensured that the boom in the traditional industries continued. Indeed it was not until 1958 that the problem re-emerged on an important scale. Aggravated by the European recession at that time, surpluses of coal were built up and the shipbuilding industry found itself with a large amount of unused capacity. These problems were apparent not only in Britain, but in Belgium and in Germany and other European countries. But to demonstrate Britain's heavy dependence on these industries it is worth noting that in 1957, the year before contraction began to set in, the United Kingdom produced 220 million tons of coal against 240 million tons for the six countries of the European Common Market combined.

From that time a changing pattern of demand and surplus capacity have ensured decline in the traditional industries. Britain has suffered from this problem more than other countries, simply because her earlier success in building up these industries and basing her prosperity on them had led to them being very strongly developed and playing a particularly important part in her economy. Within Britain,

Scotland, which in common with the north of England and South Wales had been the industrial success of the nineteenth century now had to undergo a particularly painful and difficult process of structural change. Rapid growth in new industries was necessary to make up for the decline of the old let alone make some positive contribution to the growth of gross domestic product. Moreover an environment of declining nineteenth century industry accompanied by the need for massive urban renewal is not the most conducive to new expansion. Modern light industry has shown some tendency to concentrate around the larger markets of the south.

The problem of the Scottish economy, therefore, is its structure. Though substantial improvements have been made and progress is all the while continuing, industries whose employment must on any reasonable assumptions decline still account for too large a proportion of the country's economic activity. Returning to the fallacies which were mentioned at the start of this chapter, these are not the problems of an underdeveloped agricultural region, nor is there any parallell between Scotland and the Scandinavian countries. Scotland's economy would no more become like their's as a result of political independence than her population would turn into Nordic blondes. If parallels are to be sought, the area of Europe which has most in common with Scotland economically is undoubtedly the north of England, where similar problems of structural readjustment exist. Scotland is indeed suffering from a singularly British economic sickness. In Europe the country bearing the closest similarity to this is probably Belgium, where the collapse of the Walloon coal mining industry and the difficulties of the steel firms have created a somewhat similar situation. But the area so afflicted is much more confined, and unemployment has never become a serious problem, owing to the Belgian habit of commuting either to Brussels or to France to obtain work.

If this problem is to be overcome it requires a continuing effort to readapt the Scottish economy around new forms of economic activitiy. The labour force must be re-trained or, if necessary, the population must be regrouped around centres which are suitable for the development of modern industry. Inducements of all kinds are necessary to attract new firms to Scotland and to encourage the expansion of those that are already there. Public investment must be used to improve communications and provide facilities. These are the tasks which regional policy is intended to undertake, and the effect of this policy on Scotland's economic growth forms the subject of the next chapter.

CHAPTER III

The Effect of Regional Policy

The last chapter has demonstrated the importance of achieving a faster rate of growth in Scotland and attempted to show why it has been difficult to achieve. Though Britain's growth rate has also been inadequate by the standards of some other countries, unlike Scotland's it has nevertheless been sufficient to maintain full employment. This is the main economic reason for the discontent. Its significance was not lost on the Labour party when in opposition, nor is it lost on the Nationalists now. But it was also shown that Scotland's economic performance varied throughout the twenty three years since the war, some periods being much more satisfactory than others. It is misleading, therefore, to generalise, particularly if this means judging the whole period by the standards of the late 1950s. The first decade after 1945, for example, saw much progress: Scotland's growth of output kept pace approximately with the United Kingdom's and unemployment was relatively low. From then on, however, it fell seriously behind so that by 1960 Scottish gross domestic product had risen only 10 per cent above the 1954 level. Then again in the 1960s Scotland's performance improved enabling her more or less to hold her own with the United Kingdom. While her labour force as a proportion of the British total continued to fall slightly, her income per man employed rose closer to the British average.

These changes in Scotland's performance are due to a variety of factors, but one which is of particular interest is the growing importance of regional policy. The way in which this operates therefore requires explanation. The purpose of regional policy is to try to influence the distribution of economic activity so that new industrial development is attracted or steered to particular areas. Britain has had some sort of regional policy since 1934, far longer than any other major European country, but in the early years it amounted to little. A large part of the industrial lowlands of Scotland was scheduled as a Special Area along with the North-East coast of England, West Cumberland and South Wales; and under the Special Areas Acts of 1934 and 1937 a system of loans and other financial inducements was devised to attract industry. However in a time of low economic activity and widespread unemployment in all regions, the impact on the problem was small. Only one significant measure emerged from pre-war policy, the use of Government built industrial estates where firms could obtain ready made factories and facilities. The first estate of this kind in Scotland was at Hillington, outside Glasgow. This was started in 1937 and its success led to the establishment of others.

After the war, however, a much higher priority was accorded to regional policy and three main types of measures were used. The first of these was a nationwide control of industrial development, initially by building licences and later by the system of Industrial Development Certificates established under the 1947 Town and Country Planning Act. The purpose of this was to check growth in the more prosperous parts of Britain so that it could be diverted to the Development Areas. These new Areas, which were scheduled under the 1945 Distribution of Industry Act, were similar to the Old Special Areas already mentioned but rather more extensive and included new areas such as Wrexham and parts of industrial Lancashire. In Scotland the Development Area comprised most of the industrial lowlands, Glasgow, Clydeside and much of the counties of Lanarkshire, Renfrew, Dunbarton and West Lothian. With the exception of Glasgow, which absurdly enough had been excluded pre-war, most of this area corresponded with the Old Special Area. But the Development Area was also extended to cover Dundee and in 1948 a zone around Inverness, Invergordon and Dingwall was added to act as a focal point for development in the Highlands.

Secondly, non profit-making industrial estate companies were set up under public control to build industrial estates in these Areas and to provide factories, together with appropriate services, available to rent on easy terms. Such factories might either be built to order or built in advance to a standard design and available to any tenant who chose to rent them.

Finally, in addition to these measures, financial assistance was available on application to a Treasury advisory committee which had power to negotiate loans and grants for firms setting up in Development Areas. But the assistance provided by this body was small, seldom exceeding £1 million a year for all the British Development Areas, and negotiations were liable to be protracted.

This legislation was to remain susbstantially unaltered from 1945 to 1958. It was given a high priority immediately after the war and during the years 1945–9 substantial results were obtained. This was a time when the economy was poised for expansion. Firms had had their premises destroyed or had delayed modernisation because of the war. There was therefore a surge of new investment and the economy's manufacturing output was growing at an annual rate of about 6 per cent. Circumstances were therefore favourable. But it was nonetheless a striking achievement that, in the years 1945–8, almost one half of the employment estimated to arise from new development for which Industrial Development Certificates were issued was expected to be in the Development Areas. This was a substantial proportion considering that the Areas accounted for less than 20 per cent of the British population; but, of course, even at this rate, it would have taken some time to alter the economic structure of the Areas to any substantial extent.

Unfortunately it did not continue at this rate. Balance of Payments pressure forced the Government to cut down its expenditure. Though the industrial estates continued and factories were built to order, the programme of 'advance' factories was discontinued after 1948 and not restarted again until 1959. Moreoever the return of full capacity working in the traditional industries, especially coal and shipbuilding kept unemployment low and made it almost seem as if the regional problem had disappeared. As a result, the control on development through the Industrial Development Certificate system was much relaxed. This trend was continued after

1951 under the Conservative Government which sought generally to reduce controls and restore the free market mechanism in most branches of the economy. Accordingly during these years the Development Areas received about 18 per cent of the new development taking place in Britain, as measured by employment, a share roughly in line with their population proportion. But unemployment in all the Development Areas remained low and was only 2.4 per cent of the labour force in Scotland in 1955. Although this was twice the British figure, few would have been so optimistic pre-war as to regard such low rates for either Britain or Scotland as attainable. Only Northern Ireland, with unemployment of 6.8 per cent, remained a region of obstinate labour surplus. As a result a House of Commons Select Committee in 1954 was suggesting that parts of the Areas might be descheduled.(1)

The trouble began again in the second half of the 1950s. As a result of the 1955 investment boom there was a crisis necessitating an autumn budget and a credit squeeze; in 1956 restriction was continued following the Suez Crisis, and in 1957 rumours of exchange rate adjustment between sterling and the Deutsch Mark induced speculation which resulted in Mr. Thornycroft's 7 per cent Bank Rate. As a result the economy was in recession much of the time and its rate of growth was extremely modest. This had a particularly marked effect on capital goods industry and heavy industry generally; and Scotland, along with the other Development Areas, was harder hit than the rest of Britain. As it turned out, the recession, which was purely temporary, was not the cause of the problem but aggravated a long-run trend which was beginning to make itself felt. After ten years of capacity working the shipbuilding industry had caught up with demand, stiff competition from modernised foreign yards caused order books to fall off seriously in 1956. The coal industry, after years of fuel shortage, during which exhortations to increase output were commonplace, suddenly found itself in the doldrums in the face of strong competition from oil. Huge unsold stocks built up during 1958 and it was clear that the industry would have to contract. These problems would have made themselves felt whatever the general conditions of the economy, as they did in some measure in most European countries at this time, but the recession aggravated them and prevented the slack thus created from being absorbed by development in new industries. Moreoever, as the last chapter has shown these industries were heavily represented in the economies of Scotland and the north of England and they stood to suffer most.

The Legislation since 1960

Some attempt was made to put new teeth into the legislation in 1958, but this proved to be only a stop-gap. The start of the present regional policy really dates from the Local Employment Act of 1960. As it turned out, this Act had a number of serious shortcomings and innumerable changes and modifications have been introduced since then, but it was undoubtedly a turning point in the development of British policy. Despite nearly thirty years of measures, regional development during most of the period before 1960 was a low priority item. Since 1960 it has become a more and more important part of British economic policy. Almost every year the measures have been further strengthened and extended, until they now absorb an extremely large sum of Government expenditure. No country in Europe now has such an extensive range of measures as are applied to regional policy in Britain, and none, save possibly Italy, spends so much on it.

The legislation and its numerous changes, both under Conservative and Labour Governments are far too complicated to be fully described here and I have written on this subject in detail elsewhere,(2) but a brief description is necessary to assess its importance for Scotland.

As regards the areas covered, the old Development Areas were at first replaced with a flexible system which enabled the Board of Trade to schedule any labour exchange district where unemployment of 4½ per cent of the labour force seemed likely to persist. The coverage of these Development Districts, as they were known, varied widely from year to year and tended to increase from 1961 onwards. In general the greater part of industrial Scotland was covered, as were the Highland counties.

This system proved unsatisfactory, both because the constant changes were extremely disruptive for industrial planning and because a system which is tied rigidly to unemployment percentages may preclude the building up of development in new towns and other growth points where it has the greatest chance of success. While no one would disagree that something needs to be done for unemployment blackspots, some of them, particularly on coalfields are inappropriate locations for new industry: the only hope for them may be the building up of the natural foci of economic growth in the wider region of which they form a part. In 1963 this line of thought was taken up in the well known White Paper on Central Scotland which designated eight growth areas in Central Scotland.(3) These were to remain entitled to all the advantages of Development District status, regardless of their level of employment, and to be specially favoured with public investment.

A further and more drastic change made by the Labour Government in the Industrial Development Act of 1966 carried this reasoning further. This Act introduced the new Development Areas, which are still in force today. These include the whole of Scotland, save Edinburgh, Portobello and Leith, most of Wales, the Northern region of England, Merseyside and parts of Cornwall and North Devon. The aim was to promote soundly based economic growth by enabling industry to select whatever locations within the problem regions which were best suited to their requirements. With this coverage the Development Areas included almost half of the land area of Britain and approximately 20 per cent of the population. As far as Scotland was concerned, therefore, this was the most generous treatment to date. Almost the whole country was covered, and for the first time the advantages of Development Area status applied to the Borders, Perthshire,

Dumfries, Morayshire, Nairn and much of Angus among other counties. A final modification was made to this system in 1967 with the scheduling of 'Special Development Areas'. These were small areas within the new Development Areas which had been particularly hard hit by the closure of coal mines and where especially high rates of building grants and grants to cover operating costs would be made available. Three such areas were scheduled in Scotland, in Ayrshire, Lanarkshire and Fife.

The system of control designed to steer industry to the Development Areas, which has operated since 1945, continued under the 1960 Act and was applied more stringently. Firms seeking permission to build new factories or extensions, especially in the Midlands or the South of England came under increasing pressure to locate in the Development Areas and the minimum size of development to which the control applied was lowered from 5,000 to 3,000 square feet. In 1965, for the first time, office development was made subject to control in London and the South-East and this was extended, though with less stringency, to Birmingham and the East and West Midlands Planning Regions.

The system of industrial estates continued in operation. But the various industrial estates companies were reorganised in 1960 into three large corporations, one each for England, Scotland and Wales. The programme of 'advance factories' was restarted in 1959 and was increasingly stepped up, especially under the Labour Government after 1964. Indeed many factories were built in remote locations where considerable time elapsed before tenants could be found. In consequence the Government have been criticised for letting its enthusiasm carry it too far into thinking that the mere provision of factories at highly subsidised rents could cure the unemployment of almost any area, no matter how poor a location it was in other respects for industrial development.

Financial inducements, which had been extremely limited in the period 1945–60 were expanded by stages after the 1960 Act until they are now probably the most important aspect of regional policy. First, the provision of special loans and grants, which had been obtainable from the Treasury's advisory committee, was made available under less restrictive conditions so that the committee had only to be satisfied that the proposed project was sound. The committee itself was brought under the Board of Trade and was henceforth known as the Board of Trade Advisory Committee (BOTAC).

Secondly, a number of standard grants were introduced. A building grant was provided under the 1960 Act to give firms who wished to build their own factories in Development Areas similar advantages to those who rented them on advantageous terms from the Board of Trade. At first this grant was based on a complicated formula which gave varying rates depending on building cost and the value of the factory when completed. But, since 1963, it has been at the standard rate of 25 per cent of capital cost; in certain circumstances and as of right in the Special Development Areas it may be raised to 35 per cent. Investment in plant and machinery has been assisted since 1963. At first this took the form of a standard grant at 10 per cent of cost plus a provision for 'accelerated depreciation' amounting to an important tax allowance. But since 1966 this arrangement has been replaced by investment grants paid at the rate of 40 per cent in Development Areas, compared with 20 per cent in the rest of the country (these rates were temporarily raised to 45 per cent and 25 per cent in 1967 and 1968).

Finally, subsidies on labour costs have been introduced for manufacturing industry. The Selective Employment Tax, introduced throughout Britain in 1966, taxed the service trades but gave manufacturing employers a premium of 7/6d per man employed. This premium was discontinued for the country as a whole after devaluation in the autumn of 1967, but it remains in force for the Development Areas and is therefore applicable throughout almost the whole of Scotland. In addition, the much more important Regional Employment Premium was introduced in the summer of 1967. This gives employers in manufacturing industry a premium of 30/- per man employed per week. The continuance of the scheme was guaranteed for seven years. The total labour subsidy for employees in manufacturing industry therefore stands at 37/6d per man employed per week. The cost of these two schemes is estimated at £100 million for the Regional Employment Premium and £25 million for the S.E.T. premium. The share of this expected to go to Scotland is £40 million from R.E.P. and £10 million from the S.E.T. premium, or £50 million in all.

Thus regional policy now comprises an extremely complex and wide ranging array of measures. The total cost is considerable. In 1968 this was running at an annual rate of some £250 million a year made up as shown in the table. Of this Scotland received about £100 million a year or around 40 per cent.

Approximate Annual Cost of Regional Incentives

Grants and Subsidies	**£ million**
Investment grants	65
Building grants	20
BOTAC grants	5
R.E.P.	100
S.E.T. premium	25
returnable costs:	
loans	15
factory building	15
	245

The remarkable increase in this expenditure is seen when comparing it with the past. During the 1950s the total expenditure on regional policy was normally less than £10 million a year for the whole of the United Kingdom. In 1960 it rose to £50 million but fell back again to £16 million in 1962/3. Then, if the tax provisions of the 1963 budget are included, the annual cost from 1963/4 to 1966 was in the region of £70 million to £100 million rising to £230 million to £250 million in 1967/8.

It is only fair to add, however, that firms in the Development Areas are not the only beneficiaries of this large sum of expenditure. The function of the inducements is to make business in the Areas more profitable and by doing so to encourage further expansion both from existing firms and others coming in. In so far as profits are increased, however, they are subject to corporation tax at 42 per cent, so that the Chancellor's largesse is returning to him in no small measure. Nevertheless, even allowing for this, the financial inducements at present operating are on a generous scale. The net effect, allowing for tax offsets is to reduce capital costs by some 14 - 15 per cent and to cut labour costs by about 8 per cent. This should give firms in Development Areas a significant advantage over their competitors in the rest of the country.

The effect of this policy is clearly seen in the statistics for new industrial development. Throughout the 1960s the Development Areas and Development Districts have received a higher proportion of the new employment created in Britain by factory building than they did in the 1950s. As was noted above, their share in the 1950s was around 18 per cent; between 1960 and 1962 when the Development Districts covered approximately 12 per cent of the British population they received between 20 and 30 per cent of the new employment; and in 1967 and 1968 when the new Development Areas covered 20 per cent of the British population they received around 50 per cent of the new employment created.(4) Scotland's share of this employment created by new factory building was between 16 and 20 per cent of the British total in the last two years, although the total employees in Scottish manufacturing industry amount to only 8.5 per cent of the British total.

These figures are, of course, based on the estimates of businessmen at the time of applying for Industrial Development Certificates. It may be that they exaggerate slightly the number of jobs which are likely to result. But such exaggeration, if it exists, is likely to apply to all regions and is therefore not misleading as regards the shares of new development going to Development Areas. In any case, the trend in the figures, comparing recent years with the 1950s, shows clearly that regional policy is having an impact but whether that impact is sufficient to resolve the problem is another matter. For while Scotland, in common with other Development Areas, is certainly receiving an above average share of the new development taking place in Britain, its problem stems from an above average share in declining industry. The expansion must exceed the British average by as much as the decline exceeds it for Scotland to maintain the position vis-a-vis the rest of the United Kingdom. A full assessment of the effects of regional policy therefore requires a closer look at the various indicators of Scotland's economic performance.

Returning first to the statistics of economic growth, it is possible to see some evidence of the effects of regional policy. As was pointed out earlier, in the first period, 1948 to 1954, Scotland kept pace with growth in the United Kingdom as a whole; this was the time when the traditional industries were booming and a fairly active regional policy in the 1940s had introduced some new industry. The middle period, 1954-60, was when Scotland lagged behind; and this coincides both with the decline of the traditional industries and the period when regional policy was virtually in abeyance. The final period, from 1960 on, is the most interesting. During this time the decline of the traditional industries continued unabated and obviously imposed a heavy brake on the economy; the output of coal mining and shipbuilding in 1967 were both only 65 per cent of the peak levels attained in the mid 1950s. Yet Scotland's performance was much better than in the late 1950s and in some respects outstripped the United Kingdom slightly. This must be due in large measure to the impact of regional policy. Without the special measures to steer, attract and direct new development from other parts of Britain to the Development Areas there is every reason to suppose that Scotland's growth would have lagged behind the United Kingdom in the 1960s quite as badly as it had in the second half of the 1950s. This then appears to be a modest success for regional policy. But in considering the effectiveness of this policy it must be remembered that although 1960 marked the start of the new policy many of the most powerful measures are of very recent origin dating from 1966 or 1967 and their full effect has therefore not yet had time to work itself through.

The other indicators confirm this picture, as was seen in the last chapter. Personal income per head kept pace with the United Kingdom and average earnings per man employed rose much more closely to the British average. Unemployment reached a peak figure of 135,000 in 1963 and did not rise so high again despite the severity of the measures taken to control the economy in 1966 and 1967. The main disappointment, as was shown, was the failure of employment to grow as fast as in Britain as a whole. Labour productivity rose faster than in the United Kingdom, but employment itself increased by only 2.2 per cent in the 1960s compared with 6 per cent in Britain. Regional policy therefore seems to have been much more successful in fostering the growth of output and of labour productivity than employment.

At first sight this is puzzling, and at one time it used to be argued that the measures had a capital-intensive bias. Before the introduction of R.E.P. almost all the incentives had the effect of reducing capital costs and might therefore appear to discriminate in favour of capital-using rather than labour-using industry. This is no longer the case, but it is probably inevitable that new expanding industry is capital-intensive; most modern growth industries are. The labour-intensive industries tend to be stagnant or in decline. It is therefore to be expected that an economy with an exceptionally high rate of structural change, like Scotland, will have a more rapid growth of output than employment. If more rapid employment growth is the objective, to stem the emigration and reduce the unemployment, this can best be done by stepping up the growth of production even further, not by searching around for a more labour-intensive type of industry.

It has been necessary to look at regional policy in some detail because this is the principal means by which economic growth can be fostered or slowed down in different parts of the United Kingdom. Perhaps because it is so complicated, these measures are poorly understood by the general public. In Scotland, for example, measures of general economic policy are widely criticised if they can be construed as having an adverse effect on the Scottish economy, but the substantial regional policy measures which assist the Scottish economy seldom seem to be appreciated. An example of this was the Selective Employment Tax, a measure which was unpopular throughout the country but seemed to the Scots to be designed especially for the greater tribulation of their country. Yet few realised that Scotland gets back in S.E.T. and R.E.P. premia approximately £50 million a year, a sum which comfortably exceeds all the S.E.T. payments made in Scotland.

That the operation of regional policy is not better understood is perhaps the fault of Ministers. Little has been done to publicise what Scotland is getting out of the system. Possibly Ministers may feel themselves in an awkward situation here. Too much harping on what Scotland was getting out of regional policy might make it seem that the country is dependent on charity for its existence and cause some questioning of the arrangements in those parts of England which have to foot the bill.

In reality, however, Scotland is getting no more than she deserves. If parts of an economy have spare labour resources and a capacity for growth it is right to stimulate economic activity there by releasing purchasing power and stepping up public expenditure. This is not very different from what an independent state would try to do in similar circumstances as will be seen in the next chapter. The Midlands and the South of England can only be said to be subsidising Scotland, or Wales for that matter, if the public expenditure diverted to the latter could be released in the South or the Midlands without producing inflationary pressure. Since the southern half of England has had consistently full employment, this is clearly not the case.

A more important consideration is whether regional policy has worked. This chapter has shown that it has had an impact. If much remains to be accomplished, this must be tackled by making regional policy increasingly effective, redesigning the inducements to make maximum impact and using public investment to build up centres of growth. To some the achievement so far may seem small. But Scotland's economic problem is not the kind which can be cured in a few years. To change a country's economic structure, which is what is involved, is a lengthy process likely to take decades rather than years. Present policies are achieving this change and the outlook is promising; already the declining industries are playing a smaller part and the growing industries a much larger part in the economy than they did ten years ago. As the burden of the declining sectors diminishes, so Scotland's growth rate will rise and employment will expand. With little more than 50 per cent of the labour force employed in coal mining than was in the industry in the mid fifties and a similar drop in shipbuilding, a large part of the most painful readjustment must now be past. In this respect the outlook for Scotland may be more hopeful than for the Northern region of England or for Wales. Scotland's economy is much more diversified than either of the latter, both of which are much more heavily dependent on coal, an industry which faces a continuing decline. It is noteworthy that, in contrast to Scotland, the economy of the Northern Region continued to lose ground in the 1960s and both GDP and personal income per head are now below Scottish levels.

It is not so very long ago that, thanks to Keynesian economics, Governments learnt how to manage their economies so as to avoid widespread unemployment throughout the nation in times of depression. Since the war this has been effectively controlled and British unemployment rates have been lower than at any period in the past. Even Scotland's unemployment though higher than Britain's has been low historically, certainly far lower than between the wars and probably lower than at any time before that. But the achievement of better regional balance is the task which Governments all over Europe are now attempting. No country has yet mastered this satisfactorily, but British policy has already had more effect in reducing disparities than either Italy or France have achieved, the two countries which devote most attention to regional policy in Western

Europe. What is required now is not only the continuation of this policy but its further development and strengthening. There is no other way to solve the problem.

CHAPTER IV

The Conseqences of Separation

Many people start discussion of the economics of nationalism by asking if Scotland could be self-supporting. This is an absurd question. This book has shown that Scotland has a highly industrialised economy with a gross domestic product per head which, though slightly less than England's nevertheless makes her comparable with other European countries. She is therefore among the more advanced nations of the world economically. She is clearly much wealthier than the Republic of Ireland and a thousand times more able to look after herself than Basutoland, which nonetheless manages to be independent. If Scotland becomes independent, no doubt a variety of adjustments would have to be made to her economy, some of which might be drastic and painful; but if Scotland wanted to be independent, there is obviously no question of her being unable to afford it economically.

There are two economic questions which are worth considering: the first is whether Scotland's standard of living would be reduced; and the second is whether political independence would make the solution of Scotland's economic problems easier or more difficult. The first question depends on whether Scotland is at present subsidised by England, hence the estimates of Scotland's budgetary position which have been published in the press, and on whether Scottish goods after independence would have the same access to markets outside Scotland as they do at present. This chapter will look at the budgetary position, but it is perhaps unfortunate that so much of the discussion has been focussed on this, for in some respects it is a red herring. If Scotland really has anything to gain from separation, it must be from the greater freedom she would have to fashion an economic policy more closely related to the needs of her economy. This is the crux of the matter.

Political sovereignty does not imply that economic policy can be framed regardless of external constraints; and the scope which Scotland would have for initiative in this field must therefore be carefully considered.

The Budgetary Position

Much of the discussion of the economic aspects of Scottish nationalism has centred around Scotland's contribution to Government revenue and the return she gets in public expenditure. Allegations have been made that Scotland 'puts in more than she gets back' and that most of the difficulties of the Scottish economy stem from this. On the other side it has been stated in Parliament that Government expenditure per head has been higher in Scotland over a wide range of items than it has been in the United Kingdom generally. Absence of satisfactory statistics has made the situation obscure and created a climate in which imaginative guesswork flourished and even the wildest assertions were hard to refute. Against this background the nationalist demands that 'Scotland must have control of her own purse' and that it was 'necessary to see where the money goes' have found a good deal of support. Most citizens in any state regard themselves as overtaxed, and the suggestion that the money raised in taxes is being misused in some way gains credence rather easily.

The view that the root of all evil is to be found in the budgetary position seems to be based on two serious misconceptions. First, if two states join together in union, it is not the case that what one gains the other must *necessarily* lose. Depending on the particular circumstances they may both gain economically or both lose. Even if it can be shown that one state is paying more tax revenue than the other, or receiving less expenditure in return, so that in some sense it is subsidising its partner, it still does not follow that it would be better off on its own. If it were a separate state it would have to take over on its own some of the burdens which previously were shared; and the whole position of its trade, its markets and the tariffs its export industries would have to face would quite probably be altered. These effects may greatly outweigh the cost of its taxation revenue to a united exchequer even supposing its share had been disproportionately high.

Secondly, it is not the case that if one partner state in a union contributes more to the combined exchequer than can be identified as returning in expenditure, the other must be paying less than its share. Apart from the problem of general expenditure on defence, overseas aid or foreign embassies whose benefits cannot be readily apportioned, it is highly probable that *both* partners are either contributing more or less than they get back in return. The idea that a budget should always be neatly and exactly balanced was a principle of public finance which enjoyed much support in Mr. Gladstone's day but one which was completely discredited thirty years ago in the Great Depression. Nowadays the Government may seek to obtain either a budget surplus, that is an excess of revenue over expenditure or a budget deficit, a smaller sum in revenue than it spends, depending on the exigencies of the economic situation. In times of inflation or balance of payments deficit caused by an excess of demand for goods and services over the supply available, it is now standard practice to budget for a surplus, as Mr Jenkins has done on a large scale this year. By withdrawing more money in tax than is put out in current Government expenditure, the economy's purchasing power is reduced and the level of demand cut back. In a slump the reverse procedure would be followed; a budget deficit would be used to stimulate demand and to increase purchasing power. Britain's prevailing economic condition since the war has most commonly been one of inflationary pressure and periodic balance of payments difficulty. A budget surplus has therefore commonly been the rule and it is quite possible that England, Scotland and Wales have all been contributing more in tax on certain occasions than they received in return. Obviously this does not mean that any one of them was subsidising the other.

Bearing these important qualifications in mind, it is now possible to proceed to an anlysis of the budgetary position. Many difficulties arise in this exercise, mainly as a result of

Scotland's close economic relations with the rest of the United Kingdom. On the revenue side, for example, certain taxes are collected centrally and no separate figures for Scotland are available. This applies to profits tax, corporation tax, and selective employment tax among others. Although income tax collections in Scotland are shown separately this does not cover all the incomes accruing to Scottish residents, and when companies were liable for income tax they were assessed for tax purposes in whatever region their head office happened to be. Firms with important branches in Scotland but with a head office in London would therefore be included in the English tax assessment. All this means that Government statements about the tax collected in Scotland are not particularly helpful, since for reasons of convenience or historical accident this greatly understates the tax attributable to Scotland. Similarly on the expenditure side, though much more information is now available on public expenditure in Scotland, there are several items, such as defence, administration, foreign aid, representation overseas and the servicing charge on the National Debt, which cannot readily be allocated between different parts of Britain. Thus various estimating procedures have to be resorted to which are less satisfactory than one would wish. The Government have now undertaken to produce a budgetary statement for Scotland but the task is not very much easier for them than for anyone else. Since this is a fertile area for dispute, the assumptions made for the estimates in this chapter are set out in detail in the appendix.

To start with, however, there are some key points whose validity is firmly established. On the revenue side, it was shown earlier that Scottish incomes are some ten or twelve per cent below the British average. The Family Expenditure Survey shows that expenditure per head is also below average, though by a much smaller amount. Since income and expenditure taxes form the largest part of the revenue and since we have a progressive tax system, it is therefore to be expected that the tax yield per head in Scotland is likely to be below the British average.

On the expenditure side there are certain items whose

cost per caput in Scotland must be higher than in the United Kingdom. Whereas Scotland has only 9.4 per cent of the United Kingdom population it produces about 12 per cent of the country's agricultural output and it has a high proportion of hill and upland farming. The per caput cost of agricultural subsidies is therefore likely to be higher. The road mileage per head of population is also much higher than in Britain as a whole, so that the burden of maintenance and construction costs is likely to be higher. As the last chapter showed, about 40 per cent of the expenditure on regional development comes to Scotland.

These are just some of the more obvious considerations, but they are borne out by the estimates in the Tables. Against a population ratio of 9.4 per cent, Scotland's income tax contribution works out at 8.1 per cent. Surtax is slightly higher, since unearned incomes form a larger part of personal income in Scotland than in any English regions except the South-East and the South-West. Company taxes at 8.4 per cent are based on the estimate of Scottish gross trading profits. Expenditure taxes were assumed to give a yield equal to the population ratio. This may possibly be an overestimate, since Scottish expenditure per head is only some 93 per cent of the British average; but Scottish per caput expenditure is well above the average on items such as alcohol, tobacco and consumer durables. The former of these is due to the much higher whisky consumption in Scotland, but all are heavily taxed items. Taking all the items together Central Government revenue came to £1,095 or 8.8 per cent of the United Kingdom total.

This estimate confirms as closely as possible to the definitions used in Table 41 of the National Income and Expenditure Blue Book 1968. It is much higher than the figure used by Professor Alexander in *Scotland* or that issued by the Treasury in a written Parliamentary answer.(1) This is chiefly because this estimate includes national insurance contributions and income from interest and dividends which together amount to £253 million; but it is also because the other estimates were based largely on the receipts in

TABLE V

CENTRAL GOVERNMENT REVENUE AND EXPENDITURE ATTRIBUTABLE TO SCOTLAND

Current Account 1967

£ million

	REVENUE	as a % of U.K.
Income Tax	297	8.1
Surtax	23	8.2
Profits Tax	3	8.4
Corporation Tax	98	
Overspill relief	-6	
	415	8.2
Taxes on expenditure	351	9.4
Motor vehicle duty	22	
less Export rebate	-9	
Selective employment tax	39	9.1
Stamp duties	6	6.5
Miscellaneous	8	
	417	9.2
National Insurance	179	9.4
Gross trading surplus	1	
Rent	9	
Interest and Dividends	74	10.0
	263	
TOTAL REVENUE	1,095	8.85

EXPENDITURE		as % of U.K.
Identified Public Expenditure		
Expenditure in Scotland 1967/8	1,319	11.5
of which current expenditure	937	
less Local Authority expenditure	-299	
plus Gov't grants to Local Authorities	178	
	816	
adjusted to calendar year 1967	-24	
	792	

Unallocated Expenditure:		Scottish Share Allocated		
	U.K. total	At 9.4%	At 8.8%	At 8.5%
Defence	2,388	224	210	203
External relations	326	31	29	28
Other	380	36	34	33
	3,094	291	273	264
Transfer Payments:				
Debt Interest	1,112	105	98	95
TOTAL EXPENDITURE		1,188	1,163	1,151
Surplus or Deficit		-93	-68	-56

TABLE VI

CENTRAL GOVERNMENT REVENUE AND EXPENDITURE ATTRIBUTABLE TO SCOTLAND

Capital Account 1967

£ million

REVENUE

	(a)	(b)
Current Surplus or Deficit* (Carried forward)	-93	-56
Taxes on Capital	37	37
	-56	-19
Overall balance of revenue and expenditure on current and capital amounts	-211	-174

*Based on (a) 9·4% population ratio
(b) 8·5% income ratio

EXPENDITURE

Identified Capital Expenditure:	
Gross domestic fixed capital formation 1967/8	288
Grants and other investment 1967/8	94
	382
less expenditure of Local Authorities	-213
plus capital grants to Local Authorities	18
	187
Adjusted to 1967 calendar year	-12
	175
Approximate deduction for investment by Scottish Special Housing Association, and New Town Corporation	-20
	155

Scotland, as already explained. At first sight this estimate seems to compare quite well with that published by the *Scotsman* for 1966–67.(2) Their estimated total was £913 million which, allowing for the difference in the year, seems reasonable. On the other hand the *Scotsman* estimate includes capital taxes which ought properly to be in the capital account and does not include national insurance contributions. On the basis of the definitions used here, if Scottish revenue rose at the same rate as revenue for the United Kingdom as a whole, the 1966 total would have been approximately £998 million which, with national insurance subtracted and capital taxes added would come to £865 million. Allowing for the adjustment to the financial year 1966/7 instead of the calendar year 1966 this could come to about £910 million.

The expenditure side is rather more complicated. The published figures for public expenditure in Scotland come to 11.5 per cent of the equivalent U.K. expenditure. It is therefore well above the population ratio. Moreover this identified expenditure is a high proportion, nearly 80 per cent, of the current and capital expenditure of Government and Local Authorities, excluding National Debt interest. Military defence and external relations together make up the bulk of the sum remaining. It is possible to split this into current account and capital account and, by making appropriate adjustments, to subtract the expenditure of local authorities less Government grants. This leaves a total of £792 million when adjusted to the calender year.

The remaining expenditure is for Scotland's as much as England's benefit whether or not it is disbursed in Scotland. But it can only be allocated according to some formula. The same applies to items which do not represent productive activity but are merely transfers, such as interest on the National Debt and overseas grants. One way to deal with these items is to allocate them according to the population ratio; and in that case the sum attributable to Scotland would be £396 million. This seems rather much, however, and more reasonable assumptions would be to allocate according to the proportion that Scotland's G.D.P. forms of United Kingdom

G.D.P. or Scotland's tax revenue of total tax revenue. These are 8.5 and 8.8 per cent respectively. Conceivably one could have a formula even more favourable to Scotland which allocated this expenditure on an income per head basis at a progressive rate. But according to the assumptions used here the total of Central Government Expenditure on current account varies between £1,151 million and £1,188 million.

Whatever the precise formula used for allocating the general expenditure, the position is quite clear. Scottish current account revenue forms a much lower proportion of the British total than does expenditure. There is an approximate balance between them, but no surplus to carry over to finance the capital account. In 1967 the United Kingdom current account surplus was £1,073 million; but for Scotland, depending on the assumptions, it was a deficit between –£93 million and –£56 million.

There are, of course, the capital taxes to go on the capital account and part of the expenditure may in any case be financed by borrowing. But Scotland was particularly well treated on the expenditure side of the capital account, the total figure coming to 17 per cent of the British figure on these items. To finance the bulk of the capital account by borrowing would, of course, mean that Scotland's National Debt would rise rapidly, since the items in the capital account, though investments, do not generate income to amortize the debt. The only income generating part of the capital account is Government loans. These we have not attempted to allocate to Scotland in this Table, but they could be financed by Government borrowing without leading to any long term rise in the National Debt.

Within a United Kingdom context these figures are as they should be. With a progressive tax system, it is to be expected that the richer regions of the country finance a larger share of public expenditure than the poorer ones. Public expenditure, on the other hand, should favour the regions which have need of it rather than those which can afford to pay. Scotland's *per caput* contribution towards revenue is therefore well below the British average. It is, however, surprising to see that Scotland's contribution to revenue, 8.8 per cent, is slightly higher than her share of United Kingdom income, which two years earlier, 1965, was 8.5 per cent. There is nothing unjust about this; the reason is simply that unearned income, which is more heavily taxed, forms a higher proportion of Scotland's total income than in any English region except the South-East and South-West and also that, since Scottish expenditure is much closer to the British average than income, the contribution from taxes on expenditure is high.

But while identified public expenditure in Scotland is certainly high, nationalists sometimes argue that an insufficient share of the unallocated expenditure is actually *spent* in Scotland. This is a quite separate argument. A distinction has to be drawn between the provision of grants, facilities and services through public expenditure and the use of such expenditure to provide work and employment. Without doubt Scotland's share of the former is generous, but is the latter being used to Scotland's advantage as much as it might? The nationalists' argument, as it is commonly presented, is weak. They focus attention on the unallocated expenditure, which is a small proportion of the total and consists mostly of defence; but the nationalists themselves say they would cut defence, so an independent Scotland could hardly have the advantage of this either. According to a Scottish Office statement in the most recent Quarterly Report some 7 per cent of the United Kingdom's total defence expenditure is actually spent in Scotland. But of course it must be realised that one cannot place contracts except with those capable of supplying the appropriate goods, and that a substantial part of British defence expenditure is spent neither in Scotland nor in England, but on the upkeep of troops in Germany or the purchase of weapons from the United States.

However illogical this argument, the point it raises merits serious attention and it is not simply confined to the unallocated expenditure or to defence. Public expenditure is not limited in its effects simply to the region in which grants, infrastructure or services were provided. Materials are supplied and contractors engaged from other regions to build roads or electricity stations or to provide a variety of facilities and equipment. Economic activity is thereby stimulated and employment created over a much wider area than the region for which the public investment or expenditure is provided. These spillover effects may be large, but it is not known how important they are in Scotland's case. Nor is it clear what should be done about it, or how it would be affected by independence. To try to stimulate greater self-sufficiency in fulfilling public expenditure contracts may be possible up to a point; but it is likely to be at some cost. If contracts are to be placed on a geographical basis instead of being awarded to the most economical supplier, either less equipment or facilities will be provided from a given sum of public expenditure, or the quality of what is provided may be inferior. In neither case are Scotland's interests likely to be well served by such a policy. What Scotland needs is more of the facilities which public expenditure can provide, and priority should be given to that.

None of this offers any support to the view that Scotland subsidises England, or that Scotland is getting less than its fair share of public expenditure, assertions sometimes made in nationalist circles. Indeed if Scotland were to take over responsibility for the bill which public expenditure presents in these accounts, she would either have to raise taxes sharply or engage in substantial Government borrowing. No doubt some taxes could be raised; but a substantial increase is unlikely to find favour with either politicians or the electorate, and might have a deterrent effect on industrial expansion in Scotland. To finance Government expenditure by borrowing is of course a perfectly reasonable procedure; but it is unlikely that an independent Scotland would be able to allow the situation indicated by these accounts to persist very long without taking some action to correct it. Government borrowing on this scale would flood the market with Scots securities, whose price would tend to fall owing to the excess of supply. Interest rates would rise thus making the cost of servicing the National Debt even greater. The public when confronted with a falling market of this type would be reluctant to buy and the Scottish Central Bank would have to step in to support the market, buying securities and putting out cash in return. There would thus be an increase in the money supply and, if the process continued indefinitely, an inflation probably coupled with a balance of payments deficit. Deficit financing might be all right as a short term measure to boost demand and expand the economy; but sooner or later adjustment would be necessary.

Budgetary policy is, in fact, most likely to be dictated by the balance of payments. An adverse balance of payments may be tackled in a variety of ways, but common to all of them is the need to exert some restraint on home demand. This may be done in the budget by raising Government revenue and reducing expenditure, so withdrawing purchasing power and damping down demand. In the Scottish economy, with its existing labour surplus shown both by unemployment and emigration, one would want to keep such measures to a minimum, perhaps preferring to devalue than rely solely on deflation. A Scottish devaluation poses a number of problems which are examined later. But one cannot tell whether any of these measures would be necessary without knowing the balance of payments position. The Scottish balance of payments attracts a great deal of speculation in nationalist circles, but it is impossible to estimate it satisfactorily at the moment. Figures exist for trade through Scottish ports, but by far the greatest part of Scotland's trade goes to England and this is completely unrecorded. Even if the statistics did exist, they would be of little help, since Scotland's trade could be substantially altered as a result of independence. Figures produced by the Scottish Council showing exports per head in Scotland to be higher than in the United Kingdom have attracted much attention. But these figures are no help because they are based on sales value and therefore include imported inputs. A Hillman Imp, for example, is thus shown at its full value as a Scottish export, even though many components were made in England. Moreover such figures give no guidance to the import situation, without which export figures are no indication of the balance of payments. If one wants to make a guess, and it is no more than a guess, the Family Expenditure Surveys show consumption to be a higher proportion of income in Scotland than in Britain; therefore saving must be less. But the indications are that investment in the 1960s was as high a proportion of G.D.P. in Scotland as elsewhere. And the budget, even if in bare balance on current account, was certainly in deficit overall. If the demand for consumption plus investment was higher than the resources as measured by consumption goods plus saving, it follows that Scotland was probably suffering an adverse balance of trade made good by an inflow of government and private funds from England. This would seem plausible for the 1960s, though it may not have been the case in the 1950s, when investment in Scotland was much lower and Government expenditure less generous.

But whatever the balance of payments, it is most unlikely that a Scots Government would wish to continue with the same pattern of public expenditure as exists at present. Priorities would be different. Some nationalists have spoken of repudiating the National Debt. This would save about £100 million in interest payments, but the notion is wholly absurd. The Debt was incurred in fighting wars which were as much in Scotland's defence as that of any other part of the United Kingdom. But, apart from any moral obligation, a substantial part of the Debt must be held by Scots. Are they to have their national savings or holdings of Government securities declared valueless overnight? There is no reason why an English exchequer should continue to pay Scots debt holders and if a Scots Government failed to do this it could hardly blame anyone for refusing to buy its securities in future. A much more reasonable course would be to try to get the rate of interest down so that the cost of servicing the Debt would not be so great; but the difficulties here are the province of monetary policy which will be investigated later.

By far the simplest way of dealing with the budgetary problem is to cut defence. A substantial saving could be affected here and it could be argued that this would be doing no more than recognising the realities of the existing situation. Since Scottish revenue at the moment is inadequate to cover public expenditure in Scotland (current and capital) plus an allocation of general unallocated expenditure based on income ratios, it follows that it must be making only a small contribution to the latter. The Scottish National Party seem to favour cutting defence; the implication being that a few frigates would be sufficient to keep Icelandic trawlers at bay. But there is grave danger in thinking of defence as a residual which can be cut whenever one is in a corner. If defence expenditure is useless, then it should be cut whether it can be afforded or not. But, if it is fulfilling its purpose at all effectively, defence expenditure should surely be given a much higher priority than many other items of public or private expenditure. It would be sheer nonsense to suggest that Scotland could not afford defence when other European nations with comparable living standards have substantial defence budgets. And it would be intolerable to expect England to defend the British Isles while the Scots Treasury, through savings on defence, was offering all kinds of grants and tax concessions to lure industry to Scotland instead of setting up in the Northern Region of England. So long as there is a United Kingdom it is reasonable to expect England, as the richer partner, to bear the brunt of defence expenditure. But if Scotland wants to be separate, she should be prepared to shoulder her own responsibilities.

There is therefore no painless way of tackling the budgetary problem. In reviewing the priorities, obviously the greatest importance should be attached to items of expenditure which will stimulate growth and expansion in Scotland. These contribute to further employment and a better standard of living thereby doing more in the long run for the welfare of the population than many types of social security benefit. To avoid jeopardising expansion, therefore, it might be necessary to reduce expenditure in other fields. Broadly speaking this probably means being less generous in the provision of social services. This is approximately what the Republic of Ireland has done. Since 1957 the Irish Government have developed an effective range of incentives to attract industry and encourage industrial expansion. These have had very satisfactory results. But there is no National Health Service comparable to that operating in Britain and the provision of social security generally is lower. Levels of pay in the public sector and in education are lower than in the United Kingdom and so is the provision of agricultural subsidies. Indeed it has been estimated that if British agricultural support was applied to Ireland, the Irish farmers would receive about £60 million more than they do at present.(3) Obviously Scotland is wealthier than Ireland and would be able to offer a provision of these services which was much closer to British levels than Irish; but some economies would have to be made, if tax increases were to be avoided and if Scotland was to make the sort of contribution to collective defence that other European states would be entitled to expect of her.

The Scope for an Independent Policy

The budgetary problem is essentially a problem of transition. It involves some once and for all changes, which, even if they are painful, may be overcome in time. The really important question is whether Scotland's economic problems could be more effectively tackled by an independent state than they can by the United Kingdom. This depends on whether Scotland could pursue different policies from those which the United Kingdom Government can pursue and whether these policies would be more effective.

At first sight the notion of pursuing an independent economic policy for Scotland seems very attractive. Labour shortage has been a characteristic of the greater part of the United Kingdom economy since the war, and this has undoubtedly been one of the reasons for the continuing inflationary pressure and balance of payments difficulties. As a result British Governments have repeatedly taken measures to damp down the economy and reduce effective demand. Scotland's predominant characteristic, on the other hand, has been labour surplus, as evidenced both by the unemployment rate and the emigration. It might well be argued, therefore, that the measures adopted by British Governments were quite unsuited to the conditions of the Scottish economy. It might seem that the remedy for Scotland's particular type of malaise would be to encourage expansion by all means possible, by reducing interest rates and expanding credit, and by some deficit budgetary financing if necessary. These measures would boost demand and encourage production. Of course they might produce, in the process, a serious balance of payments deficit; but the proponents of this policy would then say that the Scots merk should be devalued or some type of import controls imposed. If full employment cannot be achieved without a balance of payments deficit, this is merely evidence that the currency is overvalued; and on no account should full employment be sacrificed to the exchange rate. Devaluation would make exports cheaper, thereby stimulating demand for them, and imports more expensive, causing their replacement by home produced goods. The balance of payments would thereby be improved without sacrificing growth or full employment, which dependence on deflation alone may entail.

There are of course several respects in which this argument is too simple. In the first place unemployment and emigration rates are not sufficient proof that Scotland is free from inflationary pressure, and therefore able to follow a different policy. If the labour available in Scotland is unsuited to the employment being created, either because it lacks the right training or is in the wrong locations, then there can still be a shortage of the right kinds of labour and a consequent tendency towards inflationary wage pressure. Moreover if Scottish wage rates are kept in step with English, as they have been in the past, either by the system of collective bargaining or by the unions deliberately, then conditions in the Scottish labour market will not be the key factor in determining wage levels nor whether the country suffers wage inflation.

Secondly, it is not the case that United Kingdom economic policy has been applied without making allowances for differing regional conditions. It is true that this was not greatly taken into account until recently; and in the 1950s and early 1960s Scotland did suffer from restrictive measures which were hardly appropriate for her economic circumstances. But it is the purpose of regional policy to make this regional discrimination possible and Chapter III has already shown how regional measures have been developed in recent years. Scotland was therefore cushioned from the effects of the 1966-67 squeeze, which was otherwise the most severe imposed in Britain since the 1940s. In budgetary policy the last section of this chapter has shown that this type of discrimination is now working and that Scotland has recently had a sizeable deficit in the overall budget at a time when the United Kingdom was in surplus. Nevertheless, these qualifications do not dispense with the argument. To examine the scope which Scotland would have for independent action it is necessary to examine each of the major spheres of economic policy. But the first step is to discuss what trading relationships Scotland would have with other countries, in particular whether she would wish to make any trading agreements. For the decisions that are taken here will affect every other aspect of economic policy.

(a) Tariffs and Trade

All countries have the right to impose duties on imports. Such tariffs are commonly a convenient means of raising Government revenue, but their main purpose is to give a degree of protection to domestic industry. By raising the price of imported goods at the frontier, domestic production is made more profitable and expansion is encouraged. The danger is that such a policy tends to produce retaliation from other countries; and if everyone surrounds his country with a wall of high tariffs, the volume of world trade falls, the benefits of international specialisation are lost and every nation is worse off. It is to prevent this that the General Agreement on Tariffs and Trade (GATT) exists. Its signatories undertake to observe certain rules; and, as a result of continued effort, the world-wide level of tariffs has been progressively reduced since the war, the most recent example being the Kennedy Round.

On becoming independent, Scotland would be able to set its own tariffs, not only on imports from outside the British Isles, but also from England. But it must be borne in mind that in common with all other small countries Scotland is very heavily dependent on exports. Scottish industry whose function is limited to serving the Scottish market is a rapidly declining sector of the economy. Much of the new development which has come to Scotland since the war, including B.M.C., Rootes and all of the much valued American investment, was attracted to Scotland as a location from which to serve the British market and to a lesser extent from which to export to the Commonwealth and Europe, enjoying for the former Commonwealth Preference and for the latter the free trading advantages of the European Free Trade Association (EFTA). If these benefits were threatened in any way, not only would the investment coming into Scotland cease; but in many cases the firms already established would halt expansion or leave. A market of 5 million is too small for a large part of modern industry and it would therefore be essential to safeguard duty free access for Scottish goods to the English market. Since the Scottish and English economies have developed so closely together over such a long period, any erection of barriers between them would be disruptive. Yet the English could hardly be expected to refrain from imposing duties on Scots goods, if the Scots levied tariffs on theirs. Some type of free trade or common market arrangement is therefore essential.

The Scottish National Party have recognised this to the extent of indicating that it is not their intention to set up customs posts at the Border or to levy duties on imports from England. But the full implications of this seldom seem to be realised. First of all, Scotland can only *propose* a free trade or common market agreement, just as Britain has proposed such an arrangement to the E.E.C. It would be for England to agree or not as she saw fit. Agreement cannot be taken for granted and could be dependent on Scottish policy on a number of other matters. Failure to reach agreement on this would have a much more serious effect on Scottish industry than it would on English. Whereas the former's home market would fall from 55 million to 5 million, the latter would still have a market of 50 million even if it was denied access to Scotland. Indeed as far as English industry is concerned the Scottish market is equivalent in size to less than half the London Metropolitan Region, valuable no doubt, but not essential to survival. Scotland would therefore be in a weak bargaining position.

There is only one way to *guarantee* Scotland's freedom of access to the English market and that is by political union. Indeed it was the prospect of gaining this access and being able to trade with the English colonies that persuaded the Scots to sign the Act of Union in 1707. It is true, of course, that free trade or common market agreements can be signed without involving political union; but, whatever the *de jure* position, *de facto* such schemes can always be terminated by one of the parties when it becomes expedient to do so. And if a major power finds itself in economic difficulty, it will impose restrictions of some kind without regard to the agreement. Thus the United Kingdom contravened the E.F.T.A. agreement when it imposed the import surcharge in 1964 and the recent import deposit scheme, while within the letter of the law, nonetheless violates the spirit both of E.F.T.A. and of the Anglo-Irish Free Trade Agreement. There is no doubt, therefore that, as a guarantee of freedom of access, such schemes are a second best to political union.

There are also important differences between a common market and a free trade area. The former not only involves freedom of trade between members, but also requires harmonization of all external tariffs on imports from third countries and the establishment of common policies in agriculture, energy and various other sectors. A free trade scheme, on the other hand, while aiming to permit free trade between members, carries no obligation to harmonize external tariffs or to adopt common policies. In consequence freedom of trade has to be more restricted. Regulations have to be imposed to prevent the possibility of imports from third countries entering the Free Trade Area via the country with the lowest tariffs and from there travelling tariff free to the others. It is therefore commonly required that freedom of trade between member states be limited to those goods whose import content is below a certain proportion. Such a scheme is a great advance for the countries of the European

Free Trade Area but it is complicated and it cannot work without border control. It would not give Scotland anything like the freedom of access to the English market that she enjoys at present, and while she would technically have the right to vary her external tariffs it seems clear that this gain would be more than offset by the loss.

If political separation occurred, therefore, Scotland's interest would be best served by establishing a common market with England and Wales since, short of political union, this would give her the best guarantee of a market. Such a step, however, means losing the freedom to follow an independent tariff policy; it demands the formation of common policies in many spheres and, as will be seen, it greatly reduces the room for manoeuvre in other aspects of economic policy. Indeed there is an element of all or nothing about a common market. Agreement on tariffs and free trade is only part of what a common market is about. It makes little sense to remove tariffs if other forms of restriction and discrimination are allowed to continue. It would be quite unfair if one country lifted its tariffs and allowed more imports in only to find that its exports, though tariff free, were excluded from its partners markets by tax discrimination, subsidies, legal regulations and various restrictive practices. Indeed these latter devices may do quite as much to restrict the flow of trade as a moderate tariff system. It is therefore necessary to evolve common policies for many of the more important branches of economic policy. This the European Common Market is now seeking to do for fiscal and monetary policy, agricultural policy, regional policy, transport, monopoly and competition. And this England and Scotland would have to do in a British Common Market for exactly the same reasons.

The need for common policies is illustrated by agriculture and regional policy: agriculture has to be included, not only because it is unfair otherwise to an agricultural exporting country, but because food is such an important item in the cost of living that a country which follows a cheap food policy may be able to affect wage levels and hence the whole basis of competition. Regional policy must be included because grants given to firms in particular areas give them a competitive advantage over their rivals elsewhere. This must therefore be done according to an agreed system if the pattern of trade is not to be distorted. Most European countries now schedule as Development Areas their main depressed and underdeveloped regions, rather as Britain has done. But there is no country with virtually the whole of its territory a Development Area and eligible for grants as is now the position in Scotland. If Scotland were an independent state such an arrangement could hardly be allowed to continue.

These matters would therefore have to be decided at a supra-national level, as is now done for the European Economic Community by the Council of Ministers and the Commission in Brussels. As harmonization proceeds, more and more important issues have to be decided at this level. It is obviously unsatisfactory if decisions over such major matters rest mainly in the hands of civil servants, and some form of central political body is therefore desirable. The logic of economic union under a common market type scheme therefore points to the development of a form of political union. Even if some of the present European Governments are less than enthusiastic about this, the founders of the E.E.C. saw it quite clearly, and it was indeed their intention that economic union should be the first step towards political union. These forces would exert the same logic in an Anglo/Scottish common market; but political union obviously forms no part of nationalist thinking.

(b) Exchange Rate Adjustment

The importance of Scotland's policy on trade matters can hardly be exaggerated. A trading agreement with England, particularly of the common market type, may indeed be a necessity for the Scottish economy, but it would affect almost every other aspect of economic policy and greatly reduce the scope for independent action. An example of this is the fixing of exchange rates. Of course any sovereign state may set the foreign exchange rate for its currency as it sees fit and alter it when necessary. In many ways the Scottish situation suggests a need for devaluation. Labour surplus is commonly a sign that a country's industries are prevented by foreign competition from expanding fast enough to absorb the available labour. Although Scotland's labour surplus is mainly the consequence of structural change, devaluation by making all Scottish industries more competitive would give added boost to the expansion of growing industries and slow down the decline of some of those which were contracting, although the effect on the main contracting sectors, agriculture, coal mining and transport, would be negligible. Some of these advantages have already been apparent in Scotland since the devaluation of sterling in 1967. The test is whether normal expansionary policies can achieve full employment without causing a balance of payments deficit. If they cannot, and if it is clear that a reduction in the foreign exchange cost of exports would boost the demand for these substantially, then devaluation is indicated.

One cannot say whether Scotland should devalue the merk without knowing the balance of payments position. But it has to be recognised that there would be special difficulties about a Scottish devaluation. If Scotland had a common market arrangement with England, the English view would have to be considered. England could hardly be expected to allow tariff free entry to her market if the Scots were always going to take care so as to adjust their exchange rate as to undercut their competitors. If it was clear that Scotland was in serious balance of payments disequilibrium, no doubt a Scots devaluation could be accepted, but even then the common policy arrangements would be seriously upset and subject to renegotiation. These difficulties of exchange rate adjustment have already become apparent in the E.E.C. In the autumn of 1968 it became clear that the German mark was undervalued in respect of other currencies, especially the French franc which had been adversely affected by the inflationary wage increases earlier in the year. But to have altered the value of either currency would have seriously upset the common pricing agreement of the European agricultural policy, which had taken so long and so much hard fought compromise to work out. This was at least one of the reasons, even if not the main one, why neither country wished to change its parity.

The other problem is that devaluation to be successful requires a reduction, at least temporarily, in the real standard of living of the population. Imports become more expensive and exports have to be increased at the expense of the home consumer. This is not a policy which leads to political popularity as has been seen in Britain in 1968. In Scotland its effect would be even more striking. Being a small country, a substantial proportion of the goods consumed are imported and a devaluation would therefore produce widespread price rises. A reduction in the standard of living would be hard to bring about if Scots wage levels remained so closely related to wage levels elsewhere in Britain. Although differences in earnings exist between Scotland and England, these are mostly accounted for by differences in type of employment. National collective bargaining and common trades unions have resulted in wage rates for comparable employment being very similar. To be successful, a devaluation would have to be able to upset this. Obviously there would be intense resistance on the part of labour to such a policy. And, even if successful, it might seriously aggravate emigration from Scotland. It may be partly for these reasons that Ireland in forty years of independence has never attempted to alter the value of its currency.

(c) Monetary Policy

The type of monetary policy which Scotland's economic situation calls for is low interest rates and an expansion of credit. A reduction of interest rates would cut the cost of servicing the National Debt and thereby require less money to be levied in taxes, the problem referred to earlier. It would also reduce the cost of borrowing for industry and thereby stimulate investment in new plant and equipment. But Scotland could not reduce interest rates, or indeed operate an independent monetary policy without imposing stringent restrictions on financial flows out of

Scotland. Otherwise an attempt to reduce rates would simply result in an absence of buyers for Scottish Government paper while a better rate could be obtained on English securities. Similarly the creation of credit would have to be subject to strict control; otherwise firms would raise money in Scotland only to spend it on investment projects in England, thereby upsetting England's control of its own economy and benefiting Scotland not at all.

An independent monetary policy therefore requires all the paraphernalia of currency restrictions and control over capital movements. Would it be worth imposing such control? Almost certainly this would be seriously prejudicial to the Scottish economy. Scotland has depended since the war on a substantial inflow of foreign capital. Almost half the employment created by foreign firms in Britain since the war has gone to Scotland. Firms based in England have also contributed substantially to Scotland's growth by opening branches there. Such capital would be less likely to come if payments out of Scotland were subject to restriction. And without it the Scottish economy would have done badly indeed in the last twenty years. Moreover the Scots themselves have a substantial part of their capital invested in United Kingdom companies, regardless of whether they operate in England or Scotland. No amount of restriction in Scotland is going to ensure that this is devoted to the development of the Scottish economy. That can only be done by creating investment opportunities which are attractive to capital.

(d) Fiscal Policy

Fiscal policy has perhaps more possibilities, but even here there are difficulties. The National Party have repeatedly stated that they would not put up customs posts at the Border; yet it is clear that certain types of tax cannot be used without some sort of Border control. If purchase tax rates were significantly higher in one country than the other, there would very soon be a great traffic of goods bought in the cheaper market for distribution in the neighbour country.

Indeed this would apply to any type of tax on expenditure such as purchase tax, sales tax or value added tax. Englishmen would order their cars and refrigerators through Scottish dealers and have their whisky posted south by Scottish wine merchants. Only if the tax differences were too small to make the bother and cost of transport worthwhile would this be avoided. Wide differences in expenditure taxes could not therefore be permitted without border control.

Significant differences in personal income taxes would be easier to apply but these too could create some distortion. In an age when rapid transport systems are all the time being further developed there would be a strong incentive for the well-to-do to live in the country with less onerous tax rates and travel to work by air or other means. Some of this long distance commuting already takes place from the Channel Islands. In any case fiscal variations of this type would serve relatively little purpose as a means of developing the economy.

Probably the most fruitful area for an independent tax policy is in company taxation where it could be used as an incentive for firms to locate in Scotland without incurring unwanted anomalies. The abolition of selective employment tax for service trades or a reduced rate of corporation tax, for instance, would have a significant effect. But even regional tax rates of this type are not free of problems. As the system works at the moment the whole operations of a company are assessed for tax in whatever region the head office happens to be. If, therefore, there was a lower rate of tax in Scotland, every company would open a nominal head office in Scotland and it would then qualify for assessment at Scottish tax rates without taking any other action. If such a system was to work properly, companies operating throughout the United Kingdom would have to split up their operations to show the profitability of those plants in Scotland separately. In a firm where there were several plants in England and Scotland, all part of an integrated production process, there would be a strong incentive to avoid taxes by so arranging the books as to show the plants in the low tax country as earning the greater part of the profit.

But, in any case, this type of regionally differentiated fiscal policy is more or less what the regional policy measures are doing now. As was shown in the earlier part of this chapter, Government revenue from Scotland by no means covers expenditure, if a reasonable share of general expenditure is allocated. Far from suffering an unduly harsh fiscal policy as a result of being part of the United Kingdom it is highly improbable that an independent Scotland could treat itself so generously. Moreover this arises, at least in part, because company taxation does vary regionally. The system of accelerated depreciation introduced by Mr Maudling in 1963 amounted to a reduction in the rate of company taxation for Development Areas. The present investment grants and the Regional Employment Premium are subsidies which offset the rate of company taxation in Development Areas. It may be that this is a clumsy way of doing it, and that a differential tax rate would be better. But it is certainly a regionally differentiated fiscal policy.

An independent Scotland would be unable to offer more in public expenditure or industrial incentives than is done at present without cutting down drastically on other items; already, as we have seen, it would have a problem on its hands to bring its accounts more nearly into balance. The fiscal advantages of independence therefore largely depend on the possibility of finding taxes which are better suited to the Scottish economy; but here too, for the reasons given in this section, the scope for variation is limited.

An independent Scotland would thus face an awkward dilemma. If access to the English market, by a common market agreement or otherwise, is judged essential, freedom to follow a different economic policy from England is strictly limited. To run a separate monetary policy, devalue successfully or have a truly distinctive fiscal policy, trade at the border would have to be controlled, capital movements restricted and the migration of labour limited. This would run directly against the objectives of a common market and thereby jeopardise Scotland's trade.

The spokesmen of the National Party have been far from clear on this problem. They say they will not put up customs posts at the Border, which can only mean that they want a common market with England. Yet there is no indication that they understand the limitations that this would impose on economic policy, for they assert that independence and the alterations to policy which would then ensue would solve Scotland's economic problems. This is by far the most important economic issue raised by nationalism and it is unfortunate for Scotland that those who assert the need for constitutional change do not appear to understand it better.

Where a state consumes the vast bulk of the goods it produces, or in other words has a high degree of self-sufficiency it can control the level of production in the economy by using fiscal and monetary measures to regulate consumption and investment demand. But when a high proportion of the goods produced are sold in another state, this control is greatly weakened.

To achieve political sovereignty therefore does not mean that a state can pursue an independent economic policy regardless of what is happening elsewhere. Even if large states, such as the Soviet Union or Communist China may go their own way because they are large enough to achieve a high degree of self-sufficiency, this is not the general rule. Trade represents a growing proportion of national income in most countries and is especially high in small states. Countries such as Ireland, Denmark, Norway and New Zealand have developed particularly close trading links with the United Kingdom. A substantial part of their productive capacity is devoted to supplying the British market; and, for this reason, their future prosperity may depend almost as much on economic policies pursued at Westminster, which will allow continuing access to the British market and strengthen trade, as on any economic measures they may adopt themselves. This merely serves to illustrate how inter-dependent the modern world is economically. Complete economic sovereignty exists nowhere and certainly does not automatically come with political independence. It illustrates too the need for close international cooperation in economic matters. An independent Scotland would be similar in size to some of the countries mentioned.

It too would be heavily dependent on international trade and the extent to which it could excercise sovereignty in economic matters would be limited.

In such circumstances a small country may easily find that the larger nations pay scant regard to its interests when taking the decisions in economic policy that so much affect its prosperity. For, where there is no political representation and no constituents to satisfy, it is always difficult to ensure that vital interests are not ignored. Thus, when the United Kingdom decided to set up aluminium smelters at Invergordon, the North East coast of England and Anglesey, the Government were prepared to offer grants covering about half the capital cost plus a continuing labour subsidy, the Regional Employment Premium. The Norwegians who hitherto supplied the British market with aluminium and whose low cost hydroelectric resources make them particularly well suited for this industry, understandably complained. Free trade under E.F.T.A. was being interfered with. But their complaints and membership of E.F.T.A. availed them little against a Government which was trying to placate a disgruntled electorate.

In the same way it is clear that the New Zealand economy will receive a severe body blow if Britain joins the European Common Market, because her export trade in dairy products to Britain could be completely wiped out. Yet Britain is keen to join the E.E.C. and if the way were clear, it is unlikely that New Zealand's butter and cheese would be allowed to stand in the way. It might be a different matter if there were New Zealand members of Parliament at Westminster.

Likewise, if Scotland ceased to be part of the United Kingdom, Westminster could ride roughshod over its interests. If Industrial Development Certificates continued in use to prevent firms from setting up in the south of England, certainly no pressure would be applied to send them to Scotland. Priority would be given to England's own Development Areas. Steel mills, motor firms, aluminium smelters would therefore stay in England instead of being sent north. It would no longer matter in Westminster who won parliamentary seats in Scotland.

Whatever the constitutional arrangements, the Scottish economy must remain closely affected by the decisions of a government in London. And if, because of its need for a common market arrangement, so many of her policies must stay in line with England and her exchange rate keep in step with sterling, it would seem a grave mistake to withdraw the Scottish members of Parliament from the scene where these matters are decided. One may well doubt if Scotland's interests would be so well served by an ambassador.

CHAPTER V

The Case for Devolution

As an alternative to complete separation from England the suggestion is frequently made that Scotland should have its own parliament, or assembly of some sort, but remain within the United Kingdom. This is the home rule solution. In the form proposed it varies from an outright federal system with a regional government to an assembly which would have little power except to comment on the policies followed by the Secretary of State, whose prime responsibility would still be to the British Cabinet. The economic implications of such a change are, of course, minor compared with those that would arise in the event of independence. Rather more space is therefore given to political considerations in this chapter than its predecessors since it is on these that the case rests.

Home rule is the official policy of the Liberal Party who, under Mr Gladstone, first put it forward as the solution to the Irish question. In the early years of this century it was their intention, after setting up a parliament in Ireland to do the same in Scotland and Wales. This was killed, first by prolonged Conservative obstruction in the House of Lords, and secondly by the outbreak of war and the eventual collapse of the Liberal Party. The Labour Party were officially in favour of Scots home rule up to the Second World War but the idea was dropped by the post-war Labour leadership and it still finds no favour with them today, although individual members are strongly attracted by the idea. Indeed the most fully worked out scheme for devolution is that of John Mackintosh, Labour M.P. for Berwick and East Lothian. By contrast the Conservatives, who in the past were always opposed to any degree of home rule for Ireland, even to the extent of fomenting rebellion in Ulster, and who until recently used the title Unionist Party in Scotland, have recently found an interest in the idea. Mr

Heath in his speech of May 1968, known as the 'Declaration of Perth', put forward tentative proposals for a Scottish Assembly and announced his intention to set up a Scottish Constitutional Committee to inquire into the possibilities. This under the chairmanship of Sir Alec Douglas Home is now investigating various alternative proposals.

Some people think of the difference between home rule and the policies advocated by the Scottish National Party as merely one of degree; and in their view advocates of home rule are therefore all quasi-nationalists. But in reality the difference is quite clear-cut and is one of principle not one of degree. The Liberals, among the three traditional parties, have gone furthest in expressing themselves in favour of a Scottish Government and many therefore expected them to make some sort of electoral alliance with the nationalists. But common to all the home rule proposals is the preservation of the United Kingdom as a political unit; this the nationalists wish to destroy. It is clear that on this there can be no compromise; and the failure of any of the other parties to find common ground with the nationalists is therefore only to be expected. What is perhaps surprising is that the Liberals, with their advocacy of home rule, have not drawn more support. For if the public opinion polls are any guide, a high proportion of Scots favour home rule, while only a small minority really favour separation. The answer is probably that the difference between home rule and the policies of the National Party are not properly understood by many people; that the job on hand is to upset the present system, and the National Party seems best placed to do that; and that to the working man the Liberals are essentially a middle class party, while the National Party is entirely free of any class label.

But if there is fairly widespread support for some measure of home rule, it is clear that it raises a number of awkward constitutional problems. Little attention has been paid to these in public discussion of this question, and one has the impression that they are poorly understood. There are, of course, numerous states in the Western World who demonstrate that a federal constitution can work perfectly well. The United States, West Germany, Canada, Switzerland

and Australia all have constitutions of this type. But the difficulties are real ones and deserve to be better understood than they are. It is therefore worth considering what these are before looking in detail at the arguments in favour.

The Difficulties of a Federal System

Most of the problems arise over the division of power and responsibility between the federal and provincial authorities. While matters of defence, foreign policy and currency are clearly reserved to the federal power, tax revenue has to be shared, as has the management of the economy. In some countries this means that whichever power has the more control over the more important taxes has the greater political authority. But in any federal state the relationship between federal and provincial authority may be unstable with the powers of the federation growing at the expense of the provinces or vice versa. It is obviously very complicated if both federal and provincial authorities raise income and expenditure taxes. The work of civil servants is duplicated unnecessarily and such a system would be even more bewildering to those who have to pay tax then that which operates in Britain today. Moreover the scope for variation in tax *rates* between different parts of a federation is extremely limited. With a unified economy and no border control all the arguments of the last chapter, which were applied to an independent Scotland in a common market type union with England, apply to a federal state with equal force. It is for this reason that many federal countries have settled down with a fiscal system which gives one authority, usually the federal government, the power to levy by far the greater part of the tax revenue. An agreed share of this is then handed over to the provincial government to finance its expenditure. Such a system has the benefit of simplicity, but it could be argued that to make the provincial authorities financially dependent on the federal government downgrades them politically.

A particular difficulty arises in a state which is only a partial federation. If Scotland, for instance, was to have its own parliament, it might be expected to send less M.P.s to Westminster. Less Scottish business would be conducted there and if the country's political talent was to be concentrated in Edinburgh, it might strain resources somewhat to find 71 members to send to London. Yet, if Scotland's representation in London were cut down, the consequences could be serious. Many of the country's most important decisions would still be taken in London, not only matters of peace and war, but the main lines of economic strategy. It would matter greatly to Scotland whether the value of the currency were devalued or what particular measures were adopted to solve a balance of payments crisis, and these would inevitably be decided at Westminster. Thus if home rule means giving Scotland power to deliberate on its own local problems, roads, housing, agriculture and the like, but less influence over matters of major importance to the country's survival and prosperity, it must be rejected. To some extent these criticisms apply to Northern Ireland's consititutional position. The province's representation at Westminster was cut down after the setting up of the Stormont parliament and there is no doubt that political talent concentrates at Stormont rather than at Westminster. Indeed it is notable that Northern Ireland M.P.s seldom hold office in British Governments.

This type of problem would, of course, be avoided if Britain was a fully federal state. Each region's representation in Westminster would then be equally reduced and Parliament would only be concerned with federal matters. But since it seems unlikely that Britain will become a fully federal state, the only acceptable alternative would be for those parts of Britain which did acquire provincial governments to continue to send the full complement of M.P.s to Westminster, even if in many respects this seemed excessive.

There is another problem associated with the present British situation. Both Scotland and Wales have Secretaries of State who are ministers in the British Cabinet; they are therefore able to press their countries' interests at the highest level of Government and to ensure that no British policy is decided upon without the implications for Scotland and

Wales being properly considered. The office of these two Cabinet Ministers is unique, for none of their colleagues have their activities apportioned in the same way. Most have a department concerned with a particular range of the Governments activity, whether labour, defence, agriculture or education. These two alone base their activities on an area rather than a particular range of functions.

If Scotland had its own parliament, the office of Secretary of State in its present form would have to come to an end. No minister could be made responsible to two different parliaments, quite possibly containing different political majorities. If the Secretary of State remained a member of the British Cabinet and answerable at Westminster for his actions, then the parliament in Edinburgh would be no more than a talking-shop with no control over the executive. At the most the Secretary of State might appear before it to make policy statements; but being a member of the British Cabinet and Parliament he could not be bound by voting figures in Edinburgh. It is not hard to imagine how frustrating such a system would be. Obviously it would prove unworkable. But the only alternative is to make the Secretary of State accountable to the Scots Parliament. In that case he would have to command its confidence and be capable of obtaining majority support for the legislation he wished to enact. Since the majority party in the Scots Parliament might easily differ from that in power at Westminster, the Secretary of State could be of a different party from the British Government. He could not therefore be accountable for the Government's actions either at Westminster or in Cabinet. The question therefore is whether Scotland's interests are better served by having a minister in the British Cabinet who is specifically concerned with her affairs, or by relinquishing her Cabinet place in favour of her own parliament and government.

This is not exactly a simple matter to decide, Northern Ireland has its own parliament and government. Frequently, as at present, the Ulster Government is of a different political party to the Government at Westminster, but although this has meant that measures have had to be accepted which were not much to Stormont's liking the system has worked quite well. Doubt has been expressed, however, about the extent to which Ulster's interests are taken into account at Westminster. The Westminster attitude is apt to be that Ulster has its own administration to look after its own problems; yet home rule or no, policies decided on at Westminster affect Ulster and it would be unfortunate if its interests were overlooked. Thus at one time it was thought that the Board of Trade, in operating regional policy and diverting firms from the South of England by means of Industrial Development Certificates, would naturally give priority to trying to persuade them to accept new locations in the British Development Areas rather than interesting them in sites beyond the Irish Sea which did not come under its jurisdiction,(1) Whatever the validity of this criticism ten years ago, it seems unlikely to hold today, judging simply by the evidence. But it does illustrate the type of problem which can all too easily arise.

Home rule, then, is not a simple matter. There are snags and difficulties of which those cited above are only the most obvious. It is important to be aware of these if the adoption of an unworkable system is to be avoided. Moreover, though some of the difficulties may be overcome, others are inherent in the nature of all systems of divided government. A change should only be made, therefore, if the objections to the present system are sufficient to justify it.

The Case for Home Rule

Dissatisfaction with the present system arises for a number of reasons, but the most important is that the Scottish executive is in no direct way electorally responsible to Scotland. It is, of course, true that Scottish affairs are very largely administered from St Andrew's House in Edinburgh; and many of those that complain about the present system seem unaware of this, castigating decisions made in Edinburgh by Scots ministers on the advice of Scots civil servants as the misrule of a London Government. But apart from the fact that the Secretary of State is always a Scots

M.P. his prime responsibility is not to the Scottish people or to the other Scottish members but to the British Prime Minister who nominated him and to the British Cabinet.

This is not a criticism of any of those who have held this difficult office; it is inherent in the system. Under the United Kingdom arrangement the Prime Minister is the elected leader of both England and Scotland alike and it is incorrect to try to see the Secretary of State in any such role. He is simply a minister appointed to a department in the same way as others are nominated to the Board of Trade, Education and Health. The difficulty arises because the Secretaries of State of Scotland and Wales, alone of Cabinet Ministers, are concerned with a particular area and they therefore inevitably have a relationship with the people of that area which other ministers do not have with any part of the electorate. The fact is that the post of Secretary of State was created in response to pressure of public opinion and in some respects it is anomalous in the British system of Government. Although not electorally responsible to the Scottish people in any direct way, the Secretary of State nevertheless has to fight for Scotland's interests and try to represent her people. This seems particularly odd when Scotland votes differently from the rest of Britain and therefore has a Secretary of State from the minority party in Scotland. Thus from 1959 to 1964 Scotland had a Conservative Secretary of State although the majority of Scottish seats were Labour. This may seem no stranger than England voting Conservative and getting a Labour Government thanks to Wales and Scotland, as happened in 1950 and 1964. But the difference is that, while it is accepted that the Government is the Government of the United Kingdom as a whole, the Secretary of State is concerned with Scotland alone.

It might be thought that these niceties matter little and that the system should be judged on the quality of the administration it has produced. There is no doubt that this is high and that St Andrew's House discharges its particular role most effectively. Finding itself set up as a kind of permanent Scottish pressure group in British government, and jostling with other British ministries for a share of the funds coming from the Treasury, it has exerted itself greatly in Scotland's interest. This was shown by the high per caput figures for public expenditure in Scotland which we examined in the last chapter. Depressed parts of England are by no means so fortunate and the generous treatment which Scotland obtains is very largely due to the Scottish Office. In the same way the Edinburgh civil service, with its concern exclusively for Scottish affairs, is able to originate new ideas on a number of important Scottish questions. It was no accident that Scottish thought on the regional problem was much ahead of anything in England in the early 1960s. The application of the growth area concept originated in the White paper on Central Scotland and Scotland was well ahead in the attempt to make regional planning a workable concept.(2)

But efficient administration is not sufficient; the framework in which it is carried out is also important. Because the executive in Scotland is not directly responsible to the people it governs, they feel alienated from it. Whatever they do they have no sense of involvement in the country's administration. This for a start is unhealthy; it generates a helplessness about the country's problems and a propensity to blame them on others. The Government's efforts to tackle the economy's problems are treated with scepticism and indifference. They stand little chance of bringing about the change of spirit which is necessary for success. The contrast with Ireland, where people are interested in the efforts made on their behalf by the Government and do feel that they can involve themselves in them if they so wish, is noticeable. For this reason nationalists sometimes claim that a Scots Government would bring a vast psychological change to the country. Everyone would be 'prepared to work harder for Scotland'. One must treat all this with cautiion. But if there is any truth at all in this assertion, there is no reason why it need involve rupturing the country's links with England. Effective Scots leadership could make its contribution through a Scottish parliament within the United Kingdom quite as easily as outside. The present system makes this difficult and very few Secretaries of State have been able to overcome it.

Likewise, the absence of any sort of parliament or assembly in Scotland means that the Scottish ministers are not exposed, in a forum where the Scottish people and press are able to follow what is going on, to questions or debate nor obliged to defend their policies. In consequence, though they often govern very well, it is with scant explanation of what they are trying to do. This seems particularly apparent under the present administration and perhaps explains the low standard of public debate on many of the issues affecting Scotland at the present time. It has been one of the features of the last two years that the National Party has obtained all the publicity. Everyone is familiar with their assertions that Scotland would be better off if it was independent and with the iniquities of Selective Employment Tax, the Transport Bill and British Standard Time. But few appreciate how much Scotland is now getting out of regional policy, that the share of public expenditure coming to Scotland is so generous and that the Scottish economy has been doing much better in the 1960s than in the 1950s. It has been part of the purpose of this book to point these things out. That it is necessary to do so is evidence of the Government's incredible failure in public relations. No doubt there are various ways in which these could be improved. But the best public relations systems is a parliament where policies are debated and discussed with full reports in the press making the country aware of the alternatives open to them.

Such a system might also encourage a slightly more adventurous approach to Scots legislation. At present a great number of matters are legislated on separately for Scotland; but such legislation is usually a faithful copy of that enacted for England and Wales. In many respects this is absurd. It is costly and wasteful to legislate separately unless that legislation is different. It should be the purpose of having separate legislation in Scotland to take account of all the respects in which circumstances are different there and to what extent distinctive remedies should be applied. There are of course many matters where it is both impractical and undesirable to diverge too widely from English practice. But if a separate system is to make any sense at all one should be prepared to experiment. If this attitude were taken instead of copying legislation from England so frequently, it might be possible to try out ideas in Scotland which, if successful, England would occasionally wish to copy. Such an approach, however, is hardly possible with an executive which gets its lifeblood from Westminster and a civil service which is therefore primarily engaged in ensuring that Scotland gets its share of whatever is going rather than thinking how things might be done differently.

Finally, home rule would fit in well with the changes which must be made in local government. The reports of the Wheatley Commission on local government in Scotland and the Redcliffe-Maud Commission on England are awaited. It is clear that in both countries local government is in a most unsatisfactory condition. Modern conditions have removed all meaning from many of the boundaries; men of talent can seldom be persuaded to stand and only a minority of electors bother to vote; officials of high expertise are difficult to attract into local government service; with the growing costs of education and a limit to the revenue which can be raised from rates the system comes more and more to depend on Central Government grants. In Scotland the massive urban renewal which is necessary in Glasgow, to say nothing of the ambitious proposals for a network of urban motorways, are clearly beyond the financial resources of the city alone despite rates which are among the highest in the United Kingdom.

All are agreed that local authority boundaries need to be revised, though there is some disagreement on the nature of the revision necessary. But it seems clear that local government is at present left to grapple with problems which should be dealt with at a higher level. It is absurd for instance that major airports should be in the hands of cities when they serve the needs of a region rather than a particular urban community. Inter-city rivalry all too easily becomes apparent in the provision of facilities which it would be much better to share. In the same way the rebuilding of Glasgow is a regional rather than a purely local question. Population overspill arrangements have to be made with other towns; new towns have to be set up, and the location of industry, the provision of public investment and numerous other questions have to be settled. All of these are the province of regional planning and cannot be settled by the authorities of one city alone. Yet to involve the Central Government in questions such as these is unsatisfactory. Parliament is already seriously overloaded and so great is the pressure of business that regional matters are unlikely to get the attention they deserve.

A first step towards regional administration was taken by the Labour Government in 1964 when it set up the Regional Planning Councils and Boards, one each for Scotland and Wales and for each of the eight planning regions in England. But the position of these bodies is still rather nebulous. The members of the Council are appointed by the Government and in Scotland the Secretary of State is the chairman. They therefore lack the authority of an elected body. Nor do they have any financial powers. Their function is therefore limited to producing planning documents for their regions which they have little power to implement and which the Central Government may, and often does, ignore. It is not surprising that there has been some dissatisfaction with this situation. Members of some of the Councils have threatened to resign in protest over their inability to affect Government decisions. It is clear that this system can only be an interim arrangement and a decision must shortly be taken on the future of the Councils. The question is whether they should remain purely advisory or have limited executive functions.

A fully fledged regional government could fill a useful role here. It could not only take over the functions of the present Councils in regional planning, but it could take over from local authorities those questions which are of regional rather than local importance. If given adequate tax raising powers, it could provide the government grants necessary to bolster local authority finances and at the same time interest themselves sufficiently in local matters to ensure that they were well spent. At the other extreme, the Central Government could be relieved of some of its present functions which are primarily of a regional character, thereby economising on its time and transferring them to a forum which is able to give them more thorough consideration.

The Economic Issues

Economically home rule avoids many of the awkward questions which separation would involve. Since the political unity of the United Kingdom would be preserved, there can be no problem of Scots goods being denied access to English markets. Neither would it be necessary for the government expenditure in Scotland to be limited by the revenue raised by a Scots Government, since it is a well established principle of federal states that the richer parts subsidise the poorer. Finally, no separate balance of payments account would be kept for Scotland, the normal practice in any federal system being to treat the whole country as one unit from the point of view of foreign exchange transactions.

Ostensibly economic policy would be more closely tied to that of the London Government than if Scotland were an independent State; but in practice it might not turn out to be so. It is, of course, true that taxation could not move very far out of line; and Scotland would be expected to subscribe, in so far as she was able, to items of general expenditure such as defence which the Central Government found it necessary to undertake. But we have shown in the last chapter that, even a politically sovereign Scotland, so long as she wished a trading agreement with England, would find her ability to follow an independent economic policy extremely limited.

The merit of a federal system is that it need impose none of the burdens which an independent state should be expected to assume on its own behalf. Items of general expenditure, such as defence, can then be borne by those parts of a federal state most capable of doing so. Poorer regions are entitled to expect the same standard of social services and of public expenditure generally, as is available throughout the country. Indeed, should their need be greater, public expenditure may be higher. This is made possible by a transfer of Government revenue from the richer areas to the poorer. There are a variety of ways in which this may be done. Equalisation formulae of varying types may be applied, requiring richer provinces to contribute more in revenue to the federal exchequer than they receive back in expenditure and enabling poorer regions to receive more expenditure than their revenue contributions.

Arrangements of this nature apply to Northern Ireland at the present time, but the system in operation there is a particularly generous one. With an income per head only about 65 per cent of the British average, the yield from taxes per head is of course well below the British, or for that matter the Scottish figure. But the principle is recognised that, as a region of the United Kingdom, Northern Ireland should be entitled to the same social services, agricultural subsidies, public investments and other forms of public expenditure as apply anywhere in Great Britain. This principle is accepted so long as tax *rates* in Northern Ireland are similar to those in Britain, irrespective of their yield. Public expenditure may therefore be, and is, well in excess of revenue. Only a very small proportion of tax revenue, some 20 per cent, is levied by the Ulster Government, the power to levy the remainder being retained by Westminster; but the proceeds, apart from an agreed sum which forms a contribution towards United Kingdom general services, are paid over to Northern Ireland, since Stormont controls almost all the public expenditure in the province other than that of local authorities.

For some years Ulster Governments proceeded rather cautiously. In their anxiety to stick rigidly to the notion of comparability and not wishing to make Ulster appear too much in the red, they erred on the side of underspending. Now, however, it seems to be accepted that comparability means equality of service rather than equality of public expenditure per head. Where there is greater need, therefore, there must be greater expenditure. In particular, the provision of full employment is recognised as one of the responsibilities of the state and something which every citizen of the United Kingdom should be entitled to expect. Moreoever, since full employment has never existed in Northern Ireland and unemployment rates have remained obstinately high, it is accepted that the state must take whatever action is necessary to remedy this situation as soon as possible. The Ulster Government has interpreted this as meaning not only that it may spend more per head of the population in seeking to promote employment, but also that, in view of the gravity of the situation, the rate of grant it offers to industry may be above that given by the United Kingdom Government to firms going to the British Development Areas. Thus while firms going to the Development Areas, including Scotland, are now entitled to a 40 per cent investment grant, Ulster has been advertising grants of up to 50 per cent subject to the creation of employment in the province, and building grants at the rate of 40 per cent compared with 25 per cent in Britain. Expenditure on industrial training is also much higher.

Of course all this makes Northern Ireland's budgetary situation look very lopsided. Revenue derived from the province is all spent on public expenditure in Northern Ireland except for the small sum retained as a contribution towards United Kingdom general services. This sum, which is rather quaintly known as the 'Imperial Contribution' at present amounts to some £3½ millions a year. At times in the past it has been much higher and reached £15 million or so in some years during the 1940s and 1950s. The Imperial Contribution is paid in respect of items or services undertaken on Northern Ireland's behalf as part of the United Kingdom, but not readily allocated. These include defence, external relations, some transfer payments such as interest on the National Debt and various expenses associated with central government, the royal mint and the civil list. The Hall Committee estimated that, if these items were apportioned to Northern Ireland on a strict population ratio, the sum involved would be between £55 million and £60 million a year.(3) Compared with this the present Imperial Contribution is indeed very small.

But in any case this figure is largely meaningless owing to the devices used to keep it positive. The formal procedure is that the Imperial Contribution is fixed by the Joint Exchequer Board. In practice it is simply agreed by the two

Treasuries; and it is more or less treated as a residual for such revenue as remains over once public expenditure in the province has been covered. Of course such is the tax yield and such the rate of spending in Northern Ireland that the Imperial Contribution is inevitably small. It has, on some occasions in the past, actually been negative, the Westminster Treasury directly subsidising expenditure in Northern Ireland. And it would be negative now if Stormont had to assume full responsibility for all public expenditure in the province. Various measures have been adopted in order to keep the Contribution in the black. In the first place Stormont may borrow from Westminster in order to finance items in its capital account by loan rather than show a deficit. But, more important, Westminster has retained responsibility for paying almost all the agricultural subsidies in Northern Ireland totalling £25 - 30 million a year; and a system is in operation whereby Westminster pays some £10 - 12 million annually to help meet the exceptionally heavy cost of national insurance and social security in Northern Ireland. Recently it has been agreed that Westminster will pay a further £10 million a year to cover the cost of the new regional employment premium. None of these items are included in the list of services towards which the Imperial Contribution is paid and are therefore a straight bonus. Of course this is simply window-dressing to keep the Imperial Contribution out of the red. The fact remains that revenue raised in Northern Ireland is insufficient to meet the full bill for public expenditure in the province. If Stormont had to pay the present agricultural subsidies, the full cost of social security and an Imperial Contribution based on a population ratio it would have to raise about £100 million of additional revenue.

Northern Ireland is obviously very generously treated under this system. The need to secure agreement between the two Treasuries on the Imperial Contribution is a safeguard against Ulster taking unreasonable advantage. But parity of service means that, while unemployment persists, the Ulster Government is almost given a blank cheque on which to write whatever sum of public expenditure it thinks appropriate.

Not only is it possible to run the equivalent of a massive budget deficit, but Ulster enjoys whatever benefit there is from defence or other Central Government Services without really contributing towards them. It is plain that, if she were an independent state, this scale of public expenditure could not be maintained; and grants to industry on the present scale could only then be offered if cuts were made in other items, whether agricultural subsidies or the social services.

It is not clear whether this system could be applied to other parts of the United Kingdom without causing a breakdown. Obviously, if every region, on some pretext or other no matter how valid, ran up its public expenditure at the expense of the Imperial Contribution, the system would get out of hand and nothing would be left to provide for the central services. But if Scotland did achieve home rule this system would suit her very well. Scotland's revenue, of course, much more nearly balances the expenditure attributable to her than does Ulster's. Rearranging the items given in the last chapter (Tables V and VI on pages 57 and 58) very approximately to conform to the definitions, the results are as set out below. If identified public expenditure by the Central Government in Scotland is deducted from revenue, a balance of £185 millions is left over to go towards general unallocated expenditure such as defence, international relations and interest on the National Debt. The Imperial Contribution would therefore be positive, but of course this £185 millions is very much less than Scotland's share of these items on a strict population or income proportion. On that basis, as the figures in Chapter IV showed, Scotland's Imperial Contribution should be £400 million, using a population ratio, or £360 million, using an income ratio.

GOVERNMENT REVENUE AND EXPENDITURE IN SCOTLAND 1967

£ million

Current account	1,095	(1)	Identified Expenditure in Scotland: (1)	
Capital account	37		Current account	792
			Capital account	155
				947
		(2)	Contribution to U.K. general services(2)	185
	1,132			1,132

(1) Including agricultural support

(2) Including defence, interest on National Debt, etc.

From Great Britain's point of view the generosity of the system applied to Northern Ireland may raise some eyebrows. But in reality Northern Ireland has such special problems and is so clearly in need of catching up the rest of the country that exceptional measures are justified. If the system were applied to Scotland the rest of the country would be entitled to expect that it would always maintain a substantial Imperial Contribution and a better balance of revenue and expenditure than Ulster. A more serious disadvantage of the system is that the step by step principle has virtually removed the possibility of variations in the tax system. It is true that the minor taxes levied by Stormont are not always at the same rates as those applied in Britain, but for the rest the comparability of tax rates is regarded as necessary to justify the level of public expenditure. Yet, while not denying that it is quite impractical to vary the rates on which many of the major taxes are levied, economic conditions do vary from one region to another and some taxes, such as those designed to make more effective use of labour, may be appropriate for one area and quite unsuitable for another. The aim should therefore be to encourage the maximum flexibility consistent with the obvious limitations of levying taxes in one country.

It will be seen that the case for home rule or devolution rests largely on an assessment of political issues. The argument is a complex one and it is not surprising that people should react to it in different ways. Economically a federal state is more complicated than a unitary one, if only because the exercise of power and the control of the economy are shared, but in other respects the economic factors are neutral. If there are no serious economic obstacles, neither is there any reason to suppose that home rule would make much difference to the problems of the Scottish economy. Compared with an independent Scotland, a higher level of public expenditure could probably be maintained and British regional policy would apply to discourage industrial growth in the Midlands and South of England and encourage it in the North, in Wales and in Scotland. These are the measures which will eventually solve Scotland's economic problem if any can, but these apply so long as Scotland is part of the United Kingdom and have nothing to do with devolution. A Scottish Government might enable decisions on industrial grants to be taken more quickly, as is the case in Ulster, and make regional planning more effective. But, valuable though this is, it is marginal as far as the solution of Scotland's economic problems are concerned.

In one respect, however, there would be an advantage, Devolution would end some of the make-believe which is so much indulged in at present. It a Scots Government had control of Scotland's domestic affairs, then every piece of unpopular legislation and every real or imagined grievance could no longer be blamed on the misrule of Westminster; and it would be an entirely healthy development if the Scots came to realise that the origin of many of their problems and the solutions rest with themselves. At the same time the benefits Scotland obtains from being part of the United Kingdom would be made more explicit. Regular publication of a Scots Government's financial returns would remove all doubt about the budgetary position and show to what extent

Scotland was able to enjoy a more lavish scale of public spending through being part of the United Kingdom.

There are those, of course, who argue that to give Scotland home rule now would merely encourage its demand for independence later; that by giving the Scots their own parliament one would be providing the means for the nationalists, having won a majority, to declare a U.D.I. It may be so. But this seems too gloomy a view, and such historical parallels as there are indicate the reverse. It was Britains refusal to grant home rule, as a result of prolonged obstruction from the Conservative party, which caused Ireland eventually to demand independence. If Gladstone had succeeded in his aim to create a federal state, the British Isles might yet be politically united. To grant responsibility has the effect of making people see where their true interests lie; to withold it in the face of a strong moderate demand is to play into the hands of the extremists. It would be a tragedy indeed if Britain's mistakes over Ireland were to be repeated again in Scotland.

CHAPTER VI

Conclusion

The problem with which this book has been concerned is by no means confined to England and Scotland. Many of the world's states comprise a grouping of peoples who were either independent at some time in the past, or who retain a degree of national consciousness, as a result of a language, history or cultural inheritance, which sets them apart from the rest of the nation. They therefore have a loyalty not simply to the nation but to their own region or group as well. The strength with which this feeling may persist after many centuries of union with another people is often surprising. It caused both Ireland and Norway as well as many states in Eastern Europe, to become politically independent from their neighbours after being united since very early times. It is sometimes equally remarkable that a group of states which have had a long history of political independence may on achieving union become extraordinarily cohesive, if their people think of themselves as homogeneous. Thus the absence of separatism in both Italy and Germany is striking when it is remembered how recently each achieved unity.

That people should be proud of their heritage and aware of the distinctive aspects of their culture is, of course, desirable. If all were alike, without any variety of characteristics, the world would indeed be a dull place; and it is often an awareness of these differences and a pride in them which provides the stimulus to effort in many spheres of life. But where an awareness of these differences does exist within a state, tension may easily arise unless the institutional framework proves itself flexible enough to take account of them. The situation becomes particularly dangerous if the country's economic development has been unbalanced, favouring one group and giving another an acute grievance. It is only since the last war that governments have been able to manage the level of economic activity in their economies at all effectively, and they have still much to learn about the control of its geographical distribution. These forces have therefore given rise to problems in many states: the traditional antagonism between Flemings and Walloons in Belgium has reached a stage where it is potentially very serious; and separatist tendencies in Quebec have threatened the future of Canada. The British situation is so far much less dangerous than either of these. But it is a serious problem, and if misunderstood or mishandled, the forces which give rise to it could eventually lead to violence, as the example of Ireland has already shown.

Neither is nationalism simply the prerogative of minority groups such as the Scots or the Welsh. Of course larger countries are not subject to the same pressures. But with them nationalism takes the form of arrogance towards the characteristics of others; a tendency to regard minority groups as eccentric or absurd and foreigners as inferior; an impatience with the ways of others, indifference to their feelings and a reluctance to make enough effort to understand their point of view. At various times the English, the French and the Germans have all displayed this attitude in their dealings with small countries. And of course the more they do it, the worse the latters' sense of grievance becomes.

Nationalism in the smaller countries is a response to the fear of losing their identity. The more the Scots or the Welsh feel that what is distinctive in their way of life, their culture, language or institutions is being lost, the more nationalist they will become. Coexistence with a large and more powerful neighbour exposes them constantly to this threat. As a result, such nationalism is self-assertive, continually emphasising the points of difference.

Apart from anything which may be particularly opportune about the present political situation, which was discussed at length in chapter I, it needs little imagination to see why nationalism of this type has gained strength in recent years. Modern economic forces offer the greatest threat there has ever been to this separate identity. The development of transport has reduced the significance of distance and led to a much greater movement of people from one area to another, both as visitors and as employees, while the spread of mass production techniques and of the capital intensive industry which is associated with modern technology has caused firms to grow into large national or international concerns. The control of economic activity in Scotland and Wales is therefore increasingly exercised from outside.

It is far from easy to tackle this problem, To allow nations to fragment into smaller units is not the answer, because the whole logic of the political and economic changes which are taking place is to increase interdependence and to demand even greater cooperation. This demands larger rather than smaller political units. The emergence of the United States and Russia as the two world super-powers has reduced the scope for independent action by European states and their security can only be maintained collectively. Economic forces are tending in the same direction. The steady growth of trade, while it greatly increases prosperity, also increases the dependence of one nation on another and reduces the scope for independent action in economic policy. As this book has tried to show, the smaller the state the more it relies on such trade and therefore the more it is subject to these limitations. If Europe wants to retain enough political power to influence the course of world events and wants to be able to control its economy effectively, it stands a better chance of doing this if it can unite than as a series of nation states.

A nationalism which would balkanize the British Isles into even smaller units would seem to be the complete antithesis of this. Nationalists argue that it is not; that they too are in favour of European unity, but that they want Scotland to have a voice in the Common Market. If tiny Luxembourg can be a separate member, why not Scotland? Nationalism is nevertheless entirely against the spirit of the European Community. Whatever the attitude of some member governments at the moment, the founders of EEC saw it as leading to political union, and that is not what is in the nationalists' minds. As for having a voice, a voice is not much use unless it commands attention. Scotland's economy is so intertwined with that of England that, even with political sovereignty, its decision to join EEC would depend entirely on what England did, joining if England joined and staying out if she stayed out. This is exactly the course which Ireland, Denmark and Norway are obliged to follow at the moment, for the same reason. Scotland would thus have little bargaining power. If England did eventually get into EEC and the particular terms seemed inappropriate to Scotland, there would be little she could do about it. Any refusal to accept the agreement would be ruinous to her, but have little effect on others. Much the same would apply to agreements on the operation of particular policies inside EEC. A small nation could easiy be outvoted and forced into line. It is the major nations who can push the Community to the verge of crisis to get their interests met. It follows that in the event of British membership, Scotland's interests would be more likely to be safeguarded by Westminster taking up the cudgels on her behalf than by any other means.

But if unity for Europe is desirable, the same reasons make it necessary *a fortiori* for Britain. Many aspects of policy have to be decided for Great Britain as a whole if they are to make any sense at all. A separate Scottish defence policy is plainly an absurdity, for instance, unless it is simply a way of saying that Scotland would shelter under the defence umbrella of England and the United States without making its contribution to the collective system. It is perhaps worth reflecting that, had Scotland been independent in 1939, she would probably have tried to pursue the kind of neutralist policy which some nationalists now advocate and which the majority of nations, Norway, Denmark, Ireland, Belgium, Holland, Russia amongst others, attempted to follow then. In this she would certainly have been encouraged by Germany and, deprived of Scottish ports and naval bases, Britain would have lost the war. Of course the situation is quite different now, but the argument for such a policy is no better. The need for collective action is stronger rather than weaker. Since foreign policy and defence are so closely related, a collective system for the latter implies some conformity in the former. In fact one finds that foreign policy, in the sense of having an appreciable influence on the course of world events, is largely the province of the major powers, the smaller states playing little part except to pass resolutions at the United Nations and make useful contributions of troops to peace keeping missions.

But it is with economic policy that this book has been chiefly concerned, and its purposes will have been served if it has dispelled some fallacies and contributed to a keener awareness of the issues at stake. Of course Scotland's constitutional future is primarily a political rather than an economic question, and it must be decided as such. But political issues cannot be settled without regard to their economic consequences; and Scotland's electorate may find that a grasp of economic reality does much to increase the clarity of their political minds. Nationalism is a highly emotional subject and it is right that it should be so. Patriotism cannot be reduced to a series of purely logical deductions. But it would be a tragedy indeed if the country's future were decided in ignorance of the economic consequences or under the pretence that they were other than what they are. Although assertions abound about the effect of nationalist policies on Scotland, the standard of public debate up to now has been poor because the factual understanding of the situation is lacking. One of the more striking features of the last two years is the carefree way in which people are apparently prepared to vote nationalist more or less in ignorance of the consequences of nationalist policies. It would seem that this support is in no small measure due to dissatisfaction with the harsh economic measures adopted by the Labour Government. Yet, despite all the fuss, it was the Chancellor's aim in his post-devaluation budget to cut living standards by a mere 1 per cent compared with the previous year. Owing to continued wage pressure he has not even succeeded in that. Yet few seem to realise that the policies of a Nationalist Government might bring about a substantial drop in Scottish living standards if they were to carry out some of the measures which have been proposed and if they failed to secure satisfactory trading arrangements with England.

There seems to be few who appreciate the nature of Scotland's economic problems properly. These stem not from stagnation but from the drastic structural change which is taking place in the economy. Scotland has suffered because declining sectors played such a large part in her economy. If this loss is to be made good, and if Scotland is to achieve the same overall rate of growth as the rest of Britain, it follows that the growing industries must grow faster in Scotland than elsewhere, both to make up the leeway and to counteract their own low weighting in total ouput. Few seem to realise that in the 1960s the growing sectors in Scotland *did* grow faster than in the rest of the United Kingdom. And as a result Scotland's growth of industrial production has kept up with the British average, even if it is not yet sufficiently high to eliminate the gap in employment growth.

Neither do people seem to be aware how much better Scotland has been doing in the 1960s than she did in the second half of of the 1950s. The years 1954 to 1960 were by any standards a bad period, when every indicator of economic performance showed Scotland to be falling behind the rest of Britain. But, though the 1960s were in many respects an equally difficult period, Scotland did much better. In large measure this must be due to the substantial developments which have been made in regional policy. From being a very low priority measure until 1960, regional policy has been developed by both Conservative and Labour administrations until it now embraces a comprehensive range of measures and has a gross cost of about £250 million a year. About 40 per cent of this expenditure, or £100 million, goes to Scotland. These measures have already shown that they can make an impact on the problem, though several of them have not yet had time to have their full effect. And no doubt further developments will increase their effectiveness.

If Scotland's economic problem is to be solved, further substantial investment in new industry and new productive capacity is required. This has been the aim of regional policy, and a high proportion of this investment has been carried out by firms coming to locations in Scotland from the rest of Britain and overseas. This must continue. But it will only continue if firms in Scotland retain access to the rest of the British market and to the EFTA and Commonwealth

Preference systems. Essentially this means that whatever political arrangements are adopted, Scotland must remain part of the British Isles economy. Even leaving the new investment aside, an economic rupture is hardly possible. Scotland has been part of the United Kingdom since before the industrial revolution began and her economy has grown up within that framework. To try to break out of it now, would produce a structural upheaval which would make the structural changes of the last ten years seem very small beer. Nor could one be certain of success even in the long-run. The Scottish economy is much too small to go it alone, it cannot provide the market to make modern industry viable and it must therefore be part of a wider system.

But if access to the rest of the British market is essential for Scotland, the consequences that that entails need to be faced. In such conditions the scope to operate independent economic policies is limited. The use of tariffs and import controls is ruled out; as was argued in chapter IV, exchange rate adjustment is unlikely to be successful and monetary policy has to be kept in line unless currency restrictions are contemplated. Even room for maneovre in fiscal policy is circumscribed. The National Party has not faced up to this problem yet. And until they do their assertions hardly deserve to be taken seriously.

The same inability to face reality is evident in some of the remarks made about Scotland's budgetary position. Some nationalists argue that Scotland subsidises England. Some of those that wish to believe this will no doubt continue to do so, but the evidence gives no more support to their case than to those who believe that the earth is flat. It is clear that public expenditure in Scotland is a higher proportion of the United Kingdom total than is revenue. Indeed Government revenue derived from Scotland is barely sufficient to cover the current account expenditure, if a reasonable allocation of United Kingdom general services is made, and it leaves a large deficit on capital account. Even allowing for the necessarily approximate nature of the estimates in chapter IV, the general position is perfectly clear. But neither does this give much support to the contrary assertion sometimes heard in the south: that England would be better off if she did not have her Celtic neighbours to support, and far from standing in the way of Scottish independence she should therefore encourage it. Of course it is true that, with Scotland gone, England would have a relatively larger budget surplus than Britain does now. But she could not enjoy the difference in higher consumer spending, because the release of additional purchasing power would aggravate the inflationary and balance of payments problems from which the country suffers. It was argued in chapter I that many Scots might be persuaded to support nationalist policies if it were shown that the United Kingdom was working to the continuing disadvantage of their country. But there is no such evidence. On the contrary the maintenance of union is to the advantage of all the countries which make up the United Kingdom. Apart from purely budgetary considerations, what the smaller countries must ensure is that policies adopted at Westminster take their interests fully into account. The most effective way of achieving this is to have their representatives sitting in a United Kingdom parliament.

But this does not mean that the status quo is necessarily ideal. The forces that give rise to nationalism are serious and must not be ignored. A large body of moderate opinion is dissatisfied with the existing institutional arrangement; to ignore this would be to invite support for extreme solutions. What is required is a system which gives greater flexibility in the formation of policy and greater opportunity for involvement. In the economic sphere this is the purpose of regional policy; substantial progress in this direction has been made and further development can be expected. At the political level this would be the purpose of devolution or home rule. Perhaps the time has now come to put this into practice.

APPENDIX

Note on the Compilation of Estimates for Government Revenue and Expenditure

The Scottish estimates presented in Tables I and II of chapter 4 are intended to be comparable with those given for 1967 in Tables 41 and 42 of the Blue Book *National Income and Expenditure 1968.*

Taxes on Income

Income tax was based on the Inland Revenue surveys of personal income by region *(Reports of the Commissioners of Her Majesty's Inland Revenue).* This showed, after allowance for persons not allocated to regions, that in 1964/5 tax paid by persons in Scotland was 8.10 per cent of the total for the United Kingdom. This ratio was applied to the 1967 Blue Book figure to get an estimate for Scotland. Figures for surtax assessments in Scotland (ibidem p.109) showed Scottish surtax in 1965/6 to be £22.3 million or 8.21 per cent of the UK total. This ratio was likewise applied to the 1967 Blue Book total. Both profits tax and corporation tax were derived by assuming them to be the same proportion of the UK total as Scottish gross trading profits are of total profits. In the GDP estimates in chapter 2 this was estimated at 8.4 per cent.

Taxes on Expenditure and others

Data from the *Family Expenditure Surveys* show Scottish expenditure per household to be approximately equal to that of the UK despite lower income. But owing to the larger size of Scots households, expenditure per head is only 93 per cent of the UK average. On the other hand, Scottish expenditure per head is well above the UK average on alcohol, tobacco and consumer durables, all items which are subject to heavy rates of tax. Therefore, despite the lower aggregate expenditure per head, it was decided to assume that tax payments per head were equal to the UK average, though recognising that this might overstate revenue.

Motor vehicle licence duties are published in *Digest of Scottish Statistics* No, 32 p. 24. S.E.T. was assumed to be the same proportion to the UK total as Scottish employees, 9.13 per cent. Stamp duties were obtained from the Inland Revenue reports. National insurance was assumed to be related to the activity rate. The 1968 *Abstract of Regional Statistics* (p.10) showed this to be the same as for the UK. Income from interest and dividends is obtained mainly from loans to local authorities and public corporations. The formers' expenditure in Scotland exceeded 10 per cent of the UK total, the latter was rather less. A ratio of 10 per cent was therefore assumed.

Taxes on Capital

Death duty figures were obtained from the Inland Revenue reports. Income from capital gains tax is scarcely significant.

Current Expenditure

Table 61 of the *Digest Scottish Statistics* No. 32 gives identifiable public expenditure in Scotland. This may be compared in detail with the Treasury Analysis of Public Expenditure in Great Britain (pp. 106-9 of the 1968 Blue Book). From this it is possible to see which items remain unallocated to Scotland. Local authorities expenditure then has to be deducted and this may be obtained from *Local Government Financial Reports*; however the latest published figures were for 1966/7 and the definitions, particularly as regards the treatment of housing differ in some respects from those used in the Blue Book. Expressed as a percentage of the UK total however, it was seen that the Scottish share had remained relatively constant in recent years; this ratio was therefore applied. A similar procedure was used to obtain an estimate of grants to local authorities. Unallocated expenditure was divided to give a Scottish share in accordance with three assumptions, a population ratio of 9.4 per cent, a tax revenue ratio of 8.8 per cent and an income ratio of 8.5 per cent.

Capital Expenditure

Estimates were derived by deducting local authority expenditure from the published figure in the *Digest Scottish Statistics* in the same way as for current expenditure. There appeared to be no major items of unallocated expenditure, but the figure published in the Digest does not contain investment expenditure of certain public corporations. This was deducted in accordance with a rough estimate.

REFERENCES

Chapter II

(1) G. McCrone, *'Scotland's Economic Progress 1951-1960'*, George Allen & Unwin 1965.

(2) Lord Beveridge, *'Full Employment in a Free Society'*, George Allen & Unwin, 1944.

(3) A. D. Campbell, *'Changes in Scottish Incomes'*, *Economic Journal* 1955, and *Income*, Chapter 5 in *The Scottish Economy*, edited by A.K. Cairncross, Cambridge 1954.

(4) *The Scotsman*, Thursday July 4, 1968.

(5) *The Scottish Economy 1965-70*, Cmnd. 2864.

(6) *Report of the Commission of Inquiry into the Scottish Economy*, (Toothill Report) Scottish Council, 1961.

(7) G. McCrone, *Regional Policy in Britain*, George Allen and Unwin, 1969.

Chapter III

(1) Second Report from the Select Committee on Estimates, 1955/6: The Development Areas, HMSO, 1956.

(2) see my *Regional Policy in Britain*, op. cit.

(3) *Central Scotland: A Programme for Development and Growth*, Cmnd 2188

(4) Annual Reports of the Board of Trade on the Local Employment Acts.

Chapter IV

(1) K.J.W. Alexander, 'Scotland's National Balance Sheet', *Scotland* May 1968.

(2) *The Scotsman*, loc. cit.

(3) E.A. Attwood, 'Agricultural Developments in Ireland, North and South', *Journal of the Statistical and Social Inquiry Society of Ireland*, 1966/7.

Chapter V

(1) K.S. Isles and N. Cuthbert, *Economic Survey of Northern Ireland*, also in T. Wilson (editor) *Ulster under Home Rule*, Oxford, 1955.

(2) Cmnd. 2188 and 2864.

(3) *Report of the Joint Working Party on the Economy of Northern Ireland*, Cmnd. 1835.